Posted in the Past
Hands Across the Sea

Revealing the true stories written on postcards
by our adventurous travelling ancestors

Helen Baggott

First published 2023

Stourcastle Books
www.stourcastle.co.uk

© Helen Baggott

British Library Cataloguing in Publication Data.
A catalogue record for this book is available from the British Library.

ISBN 978-1-9161070-2-1
Printed in Great Britain

For that shy child I once knew who now realises
it's never too late to follow a dream...

Contents

Introduction

When I was researching the first two *Posted in the Past* books, I was struck by how many of the families had relatives or friends who had emigrated across the Atlantic to either America or Canada. In the early years of the 20th century more than 3 million people left the UK for Canada – escaping pollution and rising unemployment. Many were trapped in a cycle of poverty, from childhood to old age, with only brief respite being found for a young working adult before new responsibilities as a parent stretched their limited finances.

Canada needed a workforce and advertised in the UK – using postcards (handed out to visitors at exhibitions) and posters on display in post offices and shops. Many of the posters advertised specific shipping lines, especially Cunard and the Canadian Pacific Railway which owned the Empress Line that crossed the Atlantic from Liverpool to Quebec.

One postcard I researched for *Second Delivery* told the story of Rhoda Croucher and her family. Rhoda had sent a postcard to her friend in Hollingbourne, Kent. She wrote:

Just got on the boat … just going to make a start. Have seen some sights. Tremendous lot of people … some crying, some laughing.

These people were brave. They were leaving behind friends and family for what they hoped would be a better life.

After accepting how many families have emigration within their trees, another surprising fact is how many returned to the UK for visits. These were mainly working class people, but somehow they managed to afford their tickets. Even today, such a journey requires planning – and the saving of funds – and it was no different more than a hundred years ago. Perhaps some visits were to introduce children, born abroad, to their family. Of course, some returned permanently. A new country does not remove the threat of illness or unemployment. Rhoda Croucher's family would be affected by illness – and early death.

In the first two books in this series, the postcards were chosen at random – the only requirement being that the recipient could be traced to an official document that showed them at the address. This rule also applies to this book, but I have also been able to work with passenger lists to confirm, where possible, how the sender of the card connects to the recipient. This wasn't always achievable, particularly if the card was sent between friends. Beginning with that first confirmation at the address, I created 'snapshot' family trees and this allowed me to put the postcards into a context – especially useful if a visit home followed a family bereavement.

Since the *Posted in the Past* project began, I have researched hundreds of postcards and this latest volume was inspired by some of the stories I uncovered that relate to travel. While that does include emigration, not all of the cards in this book follow this subject – some postcards were sent by people on day trips and holidays, and not everyone sent home happy, carefree messages. Lizzie, on a trip to the Isle of Man, wrote:

It is that rough you cannot keep on your feet. I think I shall be washed overboard.

Many of the images of ships are depictions of the actual vessels – and this is something to bear in mind if you decide to create your own collection that follows a theme. There are examples of RMS *Titanic* labelled postcards that actually show her sister ship, RMS *Olympic*. Experts can easily identify the modifications that separate the sister ships, including the enclosing of a deck.

Some of the cards will reveal just how adventurous our ancestors were – climbing pyramids, sliding down glaciers and travelling alone across Europe. Those journeys began with a trip across the Channel – flying to Europe was yet to come. Reaching as far as pre-revolution Russia, exploring Korea before conflict tore the country apart and witnessing changes in Afghanistan that would soon reverse, ensure that some of the stories revealed are important in the context of world history.

Learning about how our ancestors travelled and explored the world has been a fascinating project within the wider one for this book. I have come across adventurous women, solo travellers at a time when it would be expected that they be accompanied by their father or husband. In contrast, today we think nothing of booking a flight abroad, or planning our trip using online resources – and even travelling solo.

When I create the snapshot family trees for my research, I never bring them up to date. You might read about someone with the same surname as, perhaps, your neighbour, but unless you know the names of your neighbour's parents, grandparents and possibly great-grandparents, you will not know if they are related. Of course, if your neighbour confirms the connection, that is their decision – it's within their control and that's just as it should be. All of the trees I have created are available on Ancestry – but they are set to private. This is because I feel it is necessary to control who has access to the additional details that might not appear in this book. Also, if a postcard recipient's grandparents had ten or so siblings each, I may not have explored each branch. It is important to explain why a person's line might have been excluded.

The genealogy resources I use are those that you will have seen on *Who Do You Think You Are?* and *A House Through Time* – census returns, marriage registers, probate records, etc. These documents are also used on the more scientific programme, *DNA Journey*. As well as these records, I have also used the 1939 register – a comprehensive list taken on the eve of the Second World War which includes dates of births, rather than the age of the person at the time a census has been taken. It's worth pointing out that the years given in some of these stories are reliant on when the records were created. As an example, the 1911 census was taken on 2 April of that year and the head of the household declared the ages of anyone at the address on that day. So, depending when a birthday fell, a year included in the stories could wrong – by up to a year.

I knew that any book written about travel would have to include the story of *Titanic* – but finding and buying a postcard sent by someone connected to the tragedy would be beyond my budget. Instead, I share two postcards of the ship that reveal their own stories.

Jacob Gibbons, a second class saloon steward, survived the tragedy. He sent a menu as a postcard from Queenstown, Ireland to a family friend in Studland, Dorset where he lived. That piece of ephemera was sold twice, eventually reaching £87,000 at auction. I grew up a few miles from Studland and went to school with one of Jacob's descendants, although I didn't discover this until decades later. That's possibly the closest I could hope to find myself to a piece of *Titanic*'s history.

Thanks to the numerous films and documentaries about the disaster, we are all able to become armchair experts about *Titanic*. Even today, programmes are made revealing new theories about how the tragedy could have been avoided or how the damage would not have proved to be fatal in slightly altered circumstances. Within days of the tragedy, newspapers were suggesting ways to improve safety on ships – including the remarkable idea of detachable decks that could be lowered as giant rafts.

The wreck of the ship was discovered in 1985 – just a few years after the film *Raise the Titanic!* was released. This story of espionage and weapons of mass destruction relied on the raising of the ship using inflatable rafts. Of course, once the actual ship had been located and filmed, it's obvious what the problem with the plot is – *Titanic* broke into two parts as she sank 2.5 miles to the seabed, making any attempts at raising her, as depicted in the film, ridiculous.

For as many films about *Titanic* that have been made, there are many more documentaries and some include detailed interviews with James Cameron, whose own obsession with the tragedy led to the production of the 1997 blockbuster, *Titanic*. The director was able to make more than 30 dives to the wreck's site, even after his film had been released. One of those later dives, in 2005, allowed him to enter a stateroom and see, via the remote camera, the fireplace and fittings that had been accurately replicated in his film, created from records kept by the ship's builder. Etched glass was still in situ along with internal windows, and glazed tiles in the Turkish bath reflected the camera's light.

My favourite film about *Titanic* has to be *A Night to Remember* (1958), based on Walter Lord's novel of the same name (published in 1956). Twenty years later, Penguin published a version that included photographs, illustrations and tables that supported the novel's content with facts. It is a wonderful book – a perfect marriage of fact and fiction. In the front matter, the publisher has included this:

Walter Lord's interest in Titanic dates back to 1926 when as a small boy he became fascinated by the subject. At the age of ten he persuaded his family to cross the Atlantic on Olympic, sister ship to Titanic, so that he could learn more about the lost liner.

John Walter Lord was born in Baltimore and lived a few miles from the docks. His mother, Henrietta née Hoffman, was a wealthy widow. Her husband had died in 1920 and she was able to take Walter and his sister Henrietta (known as Muffy) on many trips on liners – most often across the Atlantic. They appear in passenger lists on an almost annual basis – and always travelled first class.

In 1924, when Walter was only six, they sailed on SS *Orca*. A year later they sailed on *Olympic* – so Walter was definitely not ten years old (as stated above) and it seems his mother needed no persuasion. Sadly, Muffy died in 1929 but her mother and brother continued their trips, including sailing aboard RMS *Mauretania* in 1932.

The experiences Walter had during those trips were surely the inspiration for his research into *Titanic*. He might even have been aware that some of *Titanic*'s lifeboats retrieved from the sea were used, it's reported, for *Olympic*. This is perhaps unlikely, as *Olympic* was built to a slightly different design.

In later years, he appears in the passenger lists for RMS *Queen Elizabeth*, sailing to England in 1957. The list records that he planned to stay at the Dorchester Hotel in London for three weeks. This would be at the time the filming of his novel was taking place around the UK and at Pinewood Studios. The destinations of his fellow passengers were just as sophisticated and include The Ritz, Claridge's, Savoy, and so on – something they had in common with the equally glamorous passengers on *Olympic* when Walter sailed aboard the ship as a child.

The writing of Walter's novel was something of a happy coincidence. His publisher was chasing for another book that he was contractually obliged to provide. Having written a number of historical novels and considering tackling the Civil War, his editor suggested he write about *Titanic*. After all, the editor is quoted as saying, the research had already been completed, and a book could be written to satisfy the publisher. Walter warmed to the idea: 'I was ready [to write the book] without knowing it.' He added to his research by writing to regional newspapers and reaching out to survivors on both sides of the Atlantic. More than 60 contacted him, all willing to share their memories.

One of those was Edith Russell (whose family's name was originally Rosenbaum). Edith refused to join a lifeboat until her 'lucky musical pig' had been retrieved from her cabin. This scene made its way into the novel and the film.

In an interview, Edith shared this: *When Titanic was sinking and they were getting us into the lifeboats, I couldn't jump in because I was too nervous. I was clutching the pig. A sailor threw it into the lifeboat and I said, 'That does it. I'm going after it.' Then I was able to jump.*

Studland's Jacob Gibbons recalled what happened just before the ship sank: *I saw one lady … She had a mascot in the shape of a little pig which played a tune and she would not leave the ship until she had secured her treasure.*

Others reported that Edith distracted the children in her lifeboat by playing a tune from the pig. Edith bequeathed the pig to Walter Lord who in turn left it to a museum.

The success of the film adaptation was undoubtedly due to the novel's meticulous research – but there's another layer to the story. When the film's eventual producer William MacQuitty's wife was in hospital delivering their daughter, she returned home with a copy of the book (and the baby, of course). William was more familiar with *Titanic* than most – as a young boy aged six in Ireland he had witnessed one of the ship's anchors being drawn by horses to the shipyard. Later, he watched the launch and sea trials – all visible from the area where he lived.

Aboard for those sea trials as First Officer was Charles Lightoller. He would join *Titanic*'s first voyage as Second Officer and was the highest-ranking crew member to survive.

Initially it was hard for William to gain support for the making of the film. As producer he was expected to draw together all the elements necessary – including funding. To some, the story was about just another shipwreck. He argued that it was more than that; it was about the end of an era, citing, as others would do over the years that followed the tragedy, that class should not be used to assess a person's right to safety. It's well documented that those in the lower classes were prevented from finding a seat in the insufficient lifeboats. Belfast's *Titanic* memorial lists those who lost their lives in order of their 'importance'. William said that the sinking of *Titanic* was 'the end of arrogance' – future memorials, including many for the First World War, would list the names alphabetically.

Like Walter Lord, William MacQuitty met survivors, and noted that they had an extraordinary calmness, that they accepted life as it was, with an attitude of making the most of what you have, and not putting off any opportunities. Too late, were, he said, the saddest words in any language.

In this book, all of the messages on the cards have been included so you can enjoy the challenge of deciphering them. I have made some slight changes while transcribing them but you will still appreciate the tone and content as it was written.

Although you can read this book in a random order, many of the stories connect and I have created an order which I feel best tells the stories of our ancestors. I begin with the postcards of *Titanic*.

S111

Recollecting absent friends…

S061

RMS Titanic

3 May 1912
Mr Howard Moore
Sumner
Maine

Dear Howard
I am sorry I wasn't at home when you were up. But hope you will make us another visit
soon and that I shall be at home. Leon was operated on yesterday and had a piece of his
rib taken out which had started to decay.
From Aunt Ellen

Not all the postcards I research are straightforward – often a recipient might not be at the address at the time an official record has been created, as in the case of this card. So, I looked for an Ellen whose surname, before or after marriage, was Moore, who then had a relative named Leon. That led me to Ellen née Moore, who had married railway worker Francis Boynton in 1890. Their eldest son, Leon, was born the following year.

In 1880, at the age of 14, Ellen is with her grandparents and she is sick with measles – as are two of her siblings – including John who was Howard's father.

John married Lois Boynton in 1884 – Francis' sister. The couple had at least five children, including Howard who was born in 1887. Another son, Cecil, was born three years later and he died on the same day as his father in April 1913. The local newspaper, *The Ellsworth American*, carried a report that father and son had drowned as a result of a tragic accident – transporting a boom of logs. Although the exact details will never be known, John's body was found trapped within their overturned boat. Cecil's body was found much further away… *in the direction of the drift of the boom, leading to the assumption that he clung to the boom until exhausted … Mr Moore had been a hard worker and a good neighbour … Cecil was a good boy, loved and respected by all who knew him, and will be greatly missed by the young people of the place.*

Leon, who is mentioned in the postcard's message, recovered from his operation. In 1918, he appears in military passenger lists, sailing from New York. After the First World War, he married and became a railway worker.

One of the striking observations about this postcard is that it had been produced so soon after RMS *Titanic* sank. Of course, at this time it wasn't unusual for postcards to be produced using photographs of incidents and accidents; they were often available within days. With this card, it's not so much that speed but how Ellen chose to send it to her nephew, as a general postcard with no mention of the *Titanic* tragedy. Even a fortnight after the ship sunk, bodies were still being recovered and images appeared in newspapers of teams of embalmers working at sea just days before Ellen sent her card.

Of the *Titanic* postcards that are available it's not difficult to separate them into either pre- or post-tragedy. Postcards like Ellen's, that show the details of the disaster, against those showing the ship sailing through ice floes.

Companies associated with the building and stocking of the ship took advantage of its image in their pre-disaster marketing campaigns to promote their wares – Vinolia soap (offering a higher standard of toilet luxury at sea), Cooper's marmalade, and oil from the Vacuum Oil Co. Ltd. being just three. Howard Case, the American managing director of the oil company, appears in census records as living in England with his family. Fortunately, they didn't accompany him on the inaugural voyage, and he was one of those who died. Survivor accounts mention that he was helping to the end, assisting women and children into the boats. A few months later, in August, his widow Elizabeth and their children returned to America aboard RMS *Adriatic*. Elizabeth Case would later file a claim for $300,000 against the Oceanic Steam Navigation Company (ultimate owners of the White Star Line). The tragedy didn't deter her from crossing the Atlantic over the years that followed. Her daughter Helen married in England and Elizabeth would visit often, regularly appearing in passenger lists.

Nothing creates more anger in discussion groups about *Titanic* than the actual number of passengers and crew who were aboard the ship. Five postal clerks, employed by either the Royal Mail or the United States Post Office were technically neither crew nor passengers (although some records include them within the 'victualling crew' – hence the uncertainty). Their role was to sort the post during RMS (Royal Mail Service) *Titanic*'s voyage so that it might be promptly processed when the ship docked in New York. The Smithsonian National Postal Museum states that the men who worked on ships were considered to be 'the best of the best' and they 'typically sorted more than 60,000 letters a day'. Like their contemporaries who worked on *Titanic*'s sister ship, RMS *Olympic* (launched in 1910), Oscar Woody, John March, William Gwinn, James Williamson and John Smith objected to their third class accommodation and were relocated and given permission to 'dine in a private area' – where they were celebrating Oscar Woody's birthday when the ship struck the iceberg. Later, they would be seen attempting to move some of the 3,500 sacks that had been loaded at Southampton, Cherbourg and Queensland to a higher level. The men would be among the first fatalities.

BIRD'S EYE VIEW OF TRAFALGAR SQUARE AND ENVIRONS.
OCEANIC HOUSE, 1, COCKSPUR STREET, THE LONDON WEST END OFFICES OF THE WHITE STAR
AND ASSOCIATED LINES WILL BE SEEN IN THE FOREGROUND.

S062

Oceanic House, London

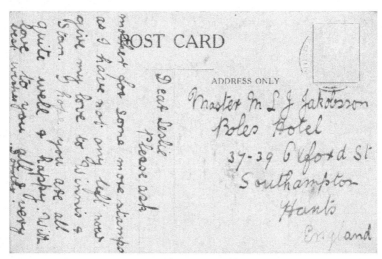

S060

RMS Titanic

Master MLJ Jakobsson
Roles' Hotel
37-39 Oxford Street
Southampton
Hants
England

Dear Leslie
Please ask Mother for some more stamps as I have not any left now. Give my love to
Winnie and Stan. I hope you are all quite well and happy. With love to you all and very
best wishes.
Dorothy

This postcard, sent to young Leslie Jakobsson, was quite likely produced before RMS *Titanic* sank – the lack of ice is a clue. Unfortunately the stamp has been removed so it is impossible to know when it was actually posted but there are clues within the family that help.

Dorothy was born in Southampton in 1898 and it is possible that like Leslie and her sister, Winifred, she was educated away from home. Leslie appears in the 1911 census as a boarder at a school in Tisbury, Wiltshire and Winifred was educated at Winchester County School for Girls, which later became the Westgate School. If she was a pupil at that school, Dorothy would have been there between about 1912 and 1916 and that is as close as we can get to the year the card was sent.

It would not have been unusual for Dorothy to have a postcard depicting *Titanic*. Her family ran the Roles' Hotel in Oxford Street, Southampton – an area known for hotels and hostels that catered for passengers and crew awaiting their passage at the nearby docks.

Mathias Jakobsson had been a sailor and was born in Finland. He married Alice Jeans in 1897 and became a naturalised citizen four years later. Alice was born in Salisbury, Wiltshire, not far from where Leslie would eventually be educated.

The couple ran the Roles' Hotel for a number of years, but Alice's connection goes further back. In 1891 she appears in the census return working for Ann Roles as a maid. Ann was from Downton in Wiltshire and perhaps this is how Alice came to be working in the hotel.

As an adult, Leslie moved away from the area and in 1939 appears in Lambeth as a minister of religion. Dorothy didn't marry and died in the 1960s in Brighton at the same address where her sister also lived. Beginning in the 1930s, Winifred was a prolific author, writing under the name Winifred Norling. Her books were written for young girls, in a similar style to Enid Blyton's boarding school sagas. Copies of her books are still available to buy and I managed to read one, *Red Herrings Unlimited* (published in 1949). As one might expect, the style and opinions are outdated, especially with regards to anyone from a lower class than the main characters, but it's possible to appreciate why she was so successful. In Brighton, she lived with another author, Baroness Marie Anna Sophie Margrete von Seydewitz. Marie mainly wrote non-fiction in German. However, I was able to track down a collection of her short stories, *Naughty Animals*, published in 1934. Aimed at young children, it's easy to imagine their delight at having the stories read to them, with the various 'naughty' animals demanding the reader hone their characterisation skills.

The Roles' Hotel – and its neighbouring businesses – would have been hugely affected by the sinking of *Titanic*. Many of the passengers stayed in accommodation in Oxford Street – also known as Titanic Street. A naval tailor at numbers 35-36 would perhaps have dressed some of the crew, although it's widely accepted that Miller & Sons, with their shop opposite Southampton's White Star Line office, would have been the first choice for many.

By the time Alice Jakobsson died in 1936, she and Mathias had left the hotel. Mathias lived for a while in Ferndown, Dorset with Dorothy and died in 1944 in nearby Wimborne.

S038

My dear Sophie
Just a few lines to let you know that it is Xmas again out here with me,
but I have never a happy one without you.
Hoping that when I go back to Belfast that you will be waiting on me,
as no other girl has taken my heart but you.
Your own sweetheart, Alex

Sadly, this postcard was sent in an envelope and there's no hope of tracing
either Sophie or Alex.

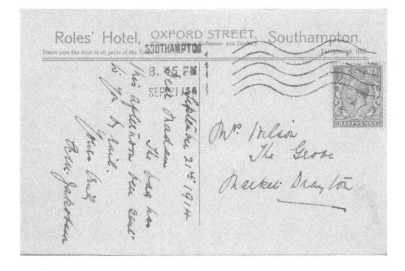

S096

Roles' Hotel, Southampton

21 September 1914
Mrs Wilson
The Grove
Market Drayton

Dear Madam
The bag has this afternoon been sent to you by rail.
Yours truly
AM Jakobsson

When I was researching the Jakobsson family for the RMS *Titanic* postcard, I decided to look for an image of Roles' Hotel, owned by the Jakobssons. This was eventually achieved nearly two years after I began researching the family. Creating searches on eBay and filtering the information down so you only see relevant hits is a great way to source cards for your own research. eBay will email you when there's a match – perhaps a family name or location. With my own family, I have found cards sent to actual addresses where my ancestors lived – at the time they were there. Although images of Roles' Hotel did pop up during the time I was searching, they were either unposted cards or the bidding went too high. The card I eventually bought went for a fraction of the price those other cards reached. I've already revealed the story of the Jakobssons but now we can look at the hotel itself. It's recorded as a temperance hotel – so strictly no alcohol available to guests. Although the rooms depicted on the card appear small, they do look very nicely presented with elaborate place settings and comfortable furniture. What makes this card extra-special to me is that it had been written by Alice Mary Jakobsson – I hadn't found any other examples of her handwriting.

Mrs Ida Wilson, née Heathcote, lived in Market Drayton with several of her adult children. Her husband, John Wilson, had died in 1900 and in earlier census returns he appears at a number of locations around the country as a landowner. He was born in Staffordshire in 1839 and lived, at various times, on the Isle of Wight (where several of his children were born), Cheltenham, Brighton and Sherborne. The family lived in Market Drayton for decades and the address appears in the probate records for several of the children. A son, Frank, died in Egypt in 1901.

It would have been lovely if a member of the family appeared in passenger lists around the time the postcard was sent and I did find some possible matches but nothing definite. The Wilson family were apparently financially secure; would Roles' Hotel have been the kind of establishment they frequented? Perhaps not.

S094

Alliance Hotel, Southampton

21 August 1913
Miss E Hancock
The Brake
St Austell
Cornwall

Dear Nell
As you see I have got so far on. This is a lovely place only about 2 minutes from station.
The Andania will leave 2.30 today. Will drop a line again at the first opportunity.
Fond love to all
Lena
XXXXX

Lena Hancock sailed on RMS *Andania* to Canada and arrived nine days after she sent the card. It's likely Nell was her sister Ellen and she was working at The Brake – a large house, owned by a brewer, Walter Hicks. Although she doesn't appear in any records at the house, the census return for 1911 confirms that Walter employed several servants. Today, the house is a care home and their website shows photos of the Hicks family taken around this time.

Lena and Ellen's parents, John and Mary, had eight children. John junior was born in Malta, Samuel in India, Ellen in Burma and the others in England. It's no surprise that their father had been in the army before returning to Cornwall to work as a clay labourer. On the family's page for the 1901 census in St Austell, all the families had members working in this industry. Clay mining had been established in Cornwall since before the last century and at one time employed almost 7,000 workers. Today, the area is known for the Eden Project – built in some of the disused clay pits.

The Alliance Hotel was just a few steps away from the Jakobssons' hotel and has a direct link to the story of RMS *Titanic*. Several passengers gave the Alliance Hotel as their address in their embarkation records.

Andania, on which Lena sailed, was only launched a month before her voyage. During the First World War it was requisitioned as a troop ship and later accommodated German prisoners of war in the Thames. It returned to civilian service in 1917, and in January 1918 left Liverpool with 40 passengers and almost 200 crew, as part of a seven-ship convoy. The ship was hit by a torpedo off Ireland and sank within a couple of hours. Although the passengers survived, a number of the crew were lost.

Records suggest that Lena, who sent the card, eventually settled in America.

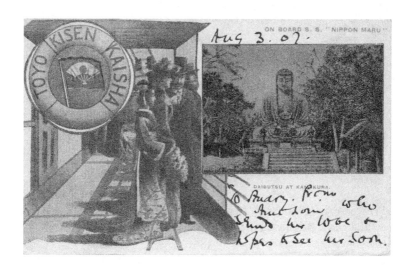

S069

S.S Nippon Maru

3 August 1907
Miss Harris
50 Campden House Court
Gloucester Walk
London W
England

To Audrey from Aunt Louisa who sends her love and hopes to see her soon.

Young Audrey was the daughter of solicitor William Cecil Harris and Rhoda née Barclay, the daughter of brewer Charles Barclay. The postcard was sent to one-year-old Audrey from her father's sister, Louisa, who was sailing aboard SS *Nippon Maru* from Hong Kong to San Francisco. In 1912 she sailed on SS *Arcadian* to New York – arriving just a few days after the sinking of RMS *Titanic*.

It's not always possible to find photographs of any of the people researched, but in 1925, Audrey appeared in *The Debutante and Court Illustrated* wearing a stunning gown matched with an ostrich feather fan.

Audrey's brother, William, married Elizabeth Coates in 1937. She was the granddaughter of politician and financier Sir Edward Coates who was also a trustee of the National Portrait Gallery. In 1903 he was elected MP for Lewisham, winning the seat for the Conservative Party.

Like her aunt, Audrey was a traveller. In 1939, her book *Eastern Visas* was published by Collins. In it, she records an epic solo journey made in 1935 across Europe to Russia and then south to Korea, Japan and China – before returning via India, Nepal and Afghanistan. She doesn't specifically reveal why she wanted to travel – other than she was drawn to China (perhaps because of her aunt's visit) and her 'indulgent father generously made it possible'.

Although much of her travels would have been 'first class', in many of the countries she visited, that didn't amount to much. She was squeezed into railway carriages, sleeping alongside strangers in their upright seats. Washing became a luxury that wasn't enjoyed every day. Aboard a steamer off Korea, she upgraded her accommodation to a communal room where she slept on the floor with only a blanket and a sawdust-filled pillow. One night she had only a male steward and another man for company. When she thought she might have the privacy to change and wash properly, she found locals would peer through doors and windows to catch a glimpse of the 'tall English woman'. They would look over her shoulder as she wrote. Often, officials would ask when checking her passport and visas, 'Where your husband?' 'Where your father?'

Her book is illustrated with photos – of her vehicle overturned on the side of a road (in reality a rough track barely suitable for the careful hooves of mules), of the landscapes and the people she met. Today, travel to some of these countries isn't permitted; international and civil wars have changed the borders forever.

Audrey wrote that Afghanistan is *modernising herself with comparative rapidity … foreign architects are building new hotels … a school of fine arts … electric light and water laid on to modern buildings.* She also mentions that she met few women. Their brief glimpse of a freer life was yet to come. That door, which was beginning to open on the wider world, would be cruelly slammed in their faces.

Perhaps Audrey's interest in overseas travel was piqued by the stories told to her by her parents. In 1932, William and Rhoda returned to England aboard SS *Chitral.* The ship's journey began at Kobe, China, stopping at Shanghai, Hong Kong, Singapore, Penang, Colombo and Bombay, then through the Suez Canal to Gibraltar and finally to Plymouth.

Audrey wrote her book in a style that hasn't dated. In the introduction, she says it is not intended as an account of *dangerous adventures, exploration or political investigation* – yet it is all these things: capturing and recording the lives and times of the places she visited. Korea would be torn in two by war and many of the historically important buildings Audrey explored were demolished by bombs.

It would be easy to imagine the book being written by an adventurous person in more modern times. Michael Palin's exploits are possibly a good comparison, although he travelled with a small crew recording his trips. He even visited North Korea, 80 years after Audrey's visit, but he was escorted and observed by officials, with limits placed on what he could see – and what he could be told. When I canvassed for suggestions of 21st century women explorers, all the responses related to journalists reporting from war zones – such is the world we now inhabit.

Audrey wasn't the only family member of her generation to have an interest in the wider world. Before the Second World War, her cousin, Ronald Harris, entered the Civil Service and was appointed to the India Office and Burma Office. Ronald would later become Private Secretary to the Secretary of the Cabinet and had a distinguished career for which he was knighted.

Not long after her book was published, Audrey married schoolteacher Edward de Mérindol Malan. His father, Walter, was a civil servant who worked in India – where he married Edward's mother, Lillian Murray, in 1900.

Edward had a fascinating career that went beyond being a teacher. In 1935 he joined the staff at Harrow School. During the Second World War he worked in the Political Intelligence Office of the Foreign Office. After the war he worked in Italy with the Royal Artillery, for which he was awarded the MBE, and then returned to Harrow. By this time he was married to Audrey, and as housemaster took charge of The Knoll. One notable pupil in his care was a prince, later to become King Hussein of Jordan.

Audrey hoped that her journey would allow her to 'understand life'. She certainly didn't want to be defined by her launch into society, by the photograph of her in her gown. One can easily imagine her meeting the parents of the children in her husband's care and having much more to offer to a conversation than polite observations.

S087

RMS Megantic

29 September 1914
Miss C Sampson
50 Bassingham Rd
Earlsfield
London
England

Dear Con
Will you write to the children as often as you can & if you want anything, money say so
& I will send it to you. Have you heard who the kind hearted Christian was who sent the
person to Cobalt to wait for us. I would like to know. I would give everything I have to get
to know. I received a card from children. They are fine.
Yours forever & ever
Matt

When I began researching this postcard I was particularly touched by the mention of children. Then, when I located Con, Constance Sampson, living at the address with her parents, I was convinced as to why children were mentioned. Con's mother, Rosina, was a foster mother and in 1911 several foster children are listed in the family's census return.

However, the truth was even more fascinating – and incredibly sadder – than I had imagined. In 1915 Con married Matthew Rutherford, a widower. His signature in the marriage register matches the handwriting on the postcard – signed as Matt. In 1911, he lived with his first wife, Emma née Flint, at 50 Bassingham Road – but within a separate household to Con's family. Matt and Emma had three daughters and he worked as a tram conductor.

Emma died in 1912 and Matt emigrated from England to Canada with his daughters in 1913, living in Cobalt where his brother, William, had settled in 1908. William's wife, Jessie, had arrived the following year.

In August 1914 Con sailed to Canada aboard SS *Grampian* for a visit, and the following month Matt enlisted with the Canadian army (11 days before the postcard was sent). At the time of enlistment his occupation is given as working in mining and he records that he has previously served with the Coldstream Guards. He appears with the Guards in the 1901 census, at the Chelsea Barracks.

When Matt and Con married in London in 1915, Matt's occupation is given as a soldier, with the 8th Highlanders. Con sailed to Canada in April 1916 and their son, Matthew, was born eight months later.

Matt died in Canada in 1918. His death certificate states that he was mentally and physically unfit from a head injury received in France and that he suffered from shellshock. A few months after his death, Con gave birth to a daughter, Agnes.

Life in Canada must have been terribly hard for Con and she returned to England with her two children. In the 1921 Canadian census, Matt's three daughters appear as the adopted children of their Uncle William in Cobalt.

Agnes, Con's daughter, would eventually marry, return to Canada and live there for a number of years.

I had hoped to find Matt in passenger lists for RMS *Megantic*. However, according to the Canadian War Museum website, the ship was used to transport troops across the Atlantic. Knowing that he was on his way to Europe to fight, adds so much to the message.

S039

Remember me, remember me. I hope you will like this.

The card was intended for a Mr Hamilton in Belfast.
It was never posted – perhaps it was sent in an envelope.

S088

RMS *Campania*

October 1910
Miss B Triggs
Lelant Downs
Lelant
Cornwall, England

Dear B
We expect to land to New York tonight. I have been ill 3 days but have got alright now.
It [is] very hot now. I hope you have written and let me know how all are going on. It seems
a long time since I left home. Eva met me at Plymouth… Some sandwiches and they were
nice. Love to all.
Alice

Beatrice Triggs and Alice were sisters – their father, tin miner Edward, and his wife, Eliza, had ten children in total and all were born in the Lelant area. Unsurprisingly, many of the sons were also involved in the tin mining industry. One son, John, worked as an electric motor driver in a mine.

The passenger lists for RMS *Campania* describe Alice as having brown hair and grey eyes – and being around 5'5" tall. She had $50 with her and worked as a cook. Her last known location in the UK was Glossop, Derbyshire and before that, she worked in St Ives, Cornwall. In 1917, at the age of 41, she married Ernest Brooks in Butte, Montana. However, the marriage records show that she was only 34. By the time Alice applied to become a naturalised citizen in 1945, her age is shown correctly as being 68. When Ernest died in 1941, his obituary noted that he had arrived in America in 1916 and had worked as a painter and decorator.

In the UK, Beatrice married Joseph Rescorla in 1911. The couple remained in the Lelant area where Joseph was a coal porter.

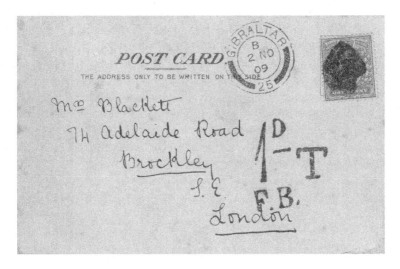

S093

SS Persia

2 November 1909
Mrs Blackett
74 Adelaide Road
Brockley
SE London

9am.
Arrived at Gibraltar this morning – sail again at 12 noon. Weather perfect – poor Sam been bad with fever since we left. Fond love to all.
KEL

Florence Apps was born in Kent in the 1860s and she married company secretary James Blackett in 1884. Florence's family were frequently involved in long trips abroad and appear in numerous passenger lists – the ship from where the card was sent was ultimately on its way to India.

The couple had at least seven children, including Grace and Irene. The sisters married civil engineers who worked overseas. Grace's husband, Arthur Taylor, appears in several lists sailing across the Atlantic to South America.

George Blackett, Florence and James' son, emigrated to Canada in 1910 but came home for visits and in 1913 returned to Canada aboard RMS *Empress of Ireland*. In 1918, he married Canadian Lucy Ivory and the couple eventually settled in Alberta.

The passenger lists for SS *Persia* are incomplete in that the first names are not always included and some passengers are listed as the 'maid of' and similar. So who might have sent the card?

James Blackett's sister, Margaret, married James Payne, a company secretary to a soap manufacturer, in 1870. Six years later, their daughter, Kate, was born. There's no record of her marrying or sailing on a ship so I don't believe it is Kate. Florence and James' children would be too young – so that rules any of them out. (Although Irene's signature in her marriage register is very similar to the handwriting on the card, she would have been around six years old on the ship!)

It's a lovely card – one of my favourites – and I always think that any card that has handwriting on the image side is more interesting because it somehow shows more of a family's history. A serious collector wouldn't want to buy such an example – mint or very clean is their usual requirement.

S001

RMS Empress of Britain

22 December 1911
Mrs Baldwin
Colley Batch
Tenbury
Worcestershire
England

We reached Halifax early this a.m. and St John's at 1.30 tonight. Breakfast at 5 a.m.
and on to the train at 7 a.m. Feeling quite alright now. A lovely smooth sea and not so
cold as we expected.
Merry Xmas & Happy New Year – though somewhat late.
KP

Kathleen and Charles Partridge had married only a few months before sailing
to Canada in 1911. RMS *Empress of Britain*'s passenger lists show that Charles
was a farmer. Despite the excitement of a new kind of life, living away from
friends and family made settling into a new community hard and less than
two years later, Kathleen (officially Lucy Kathleen) and Charles returned to
England, again sailing aboard the Canadian Pacific Line's *Empress of Britain*.
During their time away, the couple had a son, Charles junior. The family
settled in Tenbury Wells, Worcestershire, where Charles senior's family
farmed.

Kathleen was also from a farming family. Her parents, William and
Elizabeth Baldwin, owned land in Worcestershire and had, for a short time,
also tried living abroad. For them it was Rugby, Tennessee that persuaded
them to leave England and explore what was suggested would be a 'utopian'
community of like-minded people. They arrived in America some time before
1883 and settled in the town of Rugby, founded by social reformer and
author, Thomas Hughes – perhaps best known as the writer of *Tom Brown's
School Days*.

With Victorian society and laws weighted against the younger sons,
Hughes aimed to create a fairer society, and to establish a community that
didn't favour the firstborn sons (primogeniture). Being unable to inherit their
family's wealth, younger sons were destined to futures with a much reduced
status. It isn't recorded how Hughes intended to make it fairer for the
daughters of these families.

It was while visiting America for a lecture tour in the early 1870s that
Hughes began to dream of creating his 'new Jerusalem'. Together with
Boston capitalists and several wealthy Englishmen, he formed the Board of
Aid to Land Ownership Ltd. With Hughes as president, the Board employed
a team of architects to design a town from scratch – homes, hotels and a
church. There was even provision made for a drama club, tennis court and a
library (eventually stocked with 7,000 books donated by publishers from

England and America). By the end of the decade, work began – the Board owned 75,000 acres and had the option on up to five times more.

When Rugby opened in 1880, the Tabard Inn hosted almost 80 guests including dignitaries from Chattanooga, Knoxville, Cincinnati and Boston. Hughes gave a rousing speech from the inn's veranda and there was, of course, much to celebrate. However, just a few months later, Rugby suffered its first typhoid epidemic and eight residents died. The cause was traced back to the inn's well. Later, the inn would burn to the ground on two occasions and be rebuilt. Rugby needed tourists – it was trying to promote itself as a health resort, so that aspiration stalled. After 1884, visitor numbers declined and businesses suffered – guesthouses and cafes being the first. There were two main industries – a sawmill and a canning company. However, it wasn't possible to grow sufficient quantities of tomatoes to warrant the investment in the steam-operated boilers that had been brought in from Cincinnati in 1882. The canning building eventually become a successful steam-operated laundry run by an African-American family.

Hughes was a frequent visitor to Rugby, but never lived permanently in his house – Kingstone Lisle – it seems his wife refused to leave England. However, his mother, Margaret, was hugely supportive of her son and moved to Rugby in 1881 and eventually lived in Uffington House until her death. For a short while she was joined by another son, William – known by his middle name, Hastings – who later moved to Massachusetts. Hastings' daughter, Emily, was a self-taught photographer and she lived in Rugby until her grandmother's death in 1887. Many of the photographs of Rugby's early years were taken by Emily.

By the end of the 1880s the town's newspaper had ceased publication and many of the colonists had moved away – including William and Elizabeth Baldwin.

In England, William Baldwin's father was a landowner and he and his siblings were privately educated. In Rugby, William owned a large area of land in the colony and used it for farming crops. He also ran ponies and traps – renting them out to visitors, or using them as taxis to and from the railway a few miles away. The Baldwins' stay in Rugby was a short one and when they decided to return to England with their two young sons, American-born Frederick and Archer, their land was sold – one parcel alone was 200 acres. A third son, Hubert, was born in England in 1885 and Kathleen, whose postcard began this story, was born four years later. At this time, the family farmed in Herefordshire and this generation of children were also privately educated. During the First World War, Archer was awarded the Military Cross for his involvement in an attack on the Hindenburg Line. Hubert was killed at Gallipoli.

Archer would become a farmer and Conservative MP for Leominster and was knighted in 1958. His online profile says: *Baldwin was born in a log cabin* and indeed the first homes that were built in Rugby were log cabins. However, those who moved into Rugby were not necessarily the pioneers of folklore that this statement might suggest: people arriving in a covered wagon with all they possessed – although they were encouraged to bring only the essentials. While they might have been assured of a welcome, for many the conditions were harsh. Their homes had to be built, the climate wasn't kind – the area suffered droughts and harsh winters – and of course the outbreaks of typhoid meant an unsettling new life.

Rugby's eventual decline led to any uninhabited buildings falling into disrepair, but in the 1960s the Rugby Restoration Association was formed and buildings that remained were eventually listed in the National Register for Preservation.

In the first decade or so after Thomas Hughes' death, there are very few people recorded in the census returns for Tennessee as being born in England – and even fewer in the immediate area around Rugby.

S089

SS Etruria

15 July 1906
Miss L Bidgood
9 Thurlow Park Road
West Dulwich

Dear Lou
Arrived safe. The boat is lovely and everything so grand.
I will write to you when I get settled.
The dining saloon is very nice.
Love Lou

Louisa Bidgood was born in Wiltshire in 1870 where her father, George, was a labourer. Louisa's four siblings were either born in Wiltshire or in London. At the time of her sisters'– Mary and Maria – births, George was a policeman in London but he returned to Wiltshire, where he was born, and lived there with his wife, Tabitha – who was also born in Wiltshire. The family lived in several locations, including the village of Oare.

In 1911, Louisa is recorded as being a servant at the address on the card but she also returned to Wiltshire. In 1915, at the age of 42, she married widower David Hiscock from Oare. With his first wife, Anna née Tarrant, David lived at The White Hart Inn, Oare, where he was the manager. Sadly, Anna died a few months after the census was taken in 1911.

Tracing the sender of the card could have been a difficult challenge – was the sender Louise or Louisa? Passenger lists are not always transcribed accurately and fully, but I eliminated several candidates before deciding Louisa (also transcribed as Louise) Talbot was the most likely to have sent the card. In 1905 she married plasterer John Thompson and a few months later she followed him to America as Louisa Thompson. The couple eventually settled in Ohio. Of course, without an example of her writing, I can't prove that I have the correct Lou. However, Louisa Talbot's mother, Louisa Gale, was born in Oare and it seems possible that both Lous would have known each other.

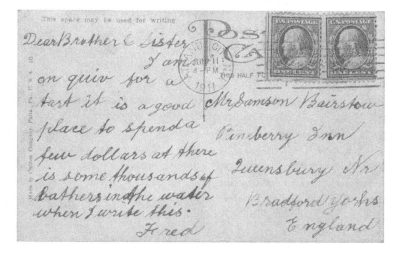

S105

Entrance to Young's New Pier
One of the Great Amusement Places of Atlantic City

11 June 1911
Mr Samson Bairstow
Pineberry Inn
Queensbury
Nr Bradford
Yorkshire
England

Dear Brother and Sister
I am on ... for a ... it is a good place to spend a few dollars and there is some thousands
of bathers in the water when I write this.
Fred

Fred Riley was the sister of Samson's wife, Sarah Riley. He was born in 1869 in Clayton, Yorkshire and, after 1901, disappears from the records I was able to access – so perhaps he settled in America. In 1901 he lived with Samson and Sarah (along with his and Sarah's parents) and was a wool porter.

Samson had a number of different jobs over the years – labourer in a brewery, cab driver and then a cab owner in 1911. At that time, Samson and Sarah's eldest child, Edith, was 13 and her day was split between attending school and working for a dressmaker. In 1939, Samson was a motor proprietor and his youngest son, Edward, was a motor driver and lived next door. Another son, Walter, was also a driver.

The pier must have been quite a sight for factory-worker Fred. It opened in 1906 and was built by Captain John Young, with – so it's claimed – the world's largest ballroom, a theatre with 4,000 seats, exhibition rooms and a roller-skating rink. Just before Fred's visit, Captain Young's mansion was built at the end of the pier, making the scene even more spectacular than could be captured by the postcard.

The Pineberry Inn was built in the mid-19th century and although it traded after the Bairstow family lived at the address, there's no mention of Samson being a licensee.

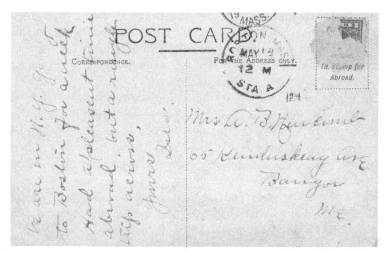

S080

RMS Carpathia

12 May 1914
Mrs AB Newcomb
65 Kenduskeag Ave
Bangor
Maine

We are in NY going to Boston for a week. Had a pleasant time aboard but a rough trip across.
Yours
?

When research is based on official records – births, deaths, etc. – inevitably, some of the stories revealed are sad and include the deaths of children.

Evelyn Hicks married Aurelius Newcomb in 1892 and the couple had at least two children. Their first child, Harold, died as an infant. Aurelius married twice, and with his first wife, Ina Abbott, he had at least four children including Henry, who died in 1904 from typhoid. Like Aurelius, after their separation, Ina remarried and with her second husband, William Nealley, she had more children including Fred who died from TB.

Aurelius was one of four children and his eldest brother, Henry, was killed in 1865, fighting in the Civil War at the Battle of Hatcher's Run, Petersburg, Virginia. He was only 19. Families in the UK often have a connection with the First World War; the same is true of the Civil War in American families. The early 1860s aren't that far away. You don't have to go back many generations to discover someone who fought or was killed during this war. Not all the losses were through injury – many died from disease: smallpox, diarrhoea, pneumonia, typhoid or diphtheria. The Battle of Hatcher's Run was fought in February 1865 – so we can add cold weather to the conditions endured.

A directory from 1914 shows that Aurelius was a carpenter. According to others' research, the Newcomb family can trace their ancestry to the *Mayflower*. I can't verify that claim. Applying for membership of the Mayflower Society is a robust process that takes months of investigation. More than 30 million people are recorded as being descended from someone who sailed on the ship.

S090

RMS Orsova

26 September 1914
Miss and the Masters Willmoth
181 Watling Street Road
Fulwood
Preston
Lancashire

This is the ship in which I am sailing back to Uncle Les in Australia. The sea is calm now and I hope it will remain so. I am sorry I didn't see you all again. Don't forget me.
Much love
Auntie Flo

Auntie Flo was writing to the children of her brother, Walter Willmoth, an accountant who was born in Ireland in 1876. His children were Dorothy, Walter and Alan.

Florence and Walter senior were two of John Willmoth's eight children – all born around the UK where John served in the army. In the 1891 census his occupation is given as quarter-master sergeant.

Auntie Flo was born in 1873 in Wales. In 1904 she is listed as a student studying at the University of London. She often appears in passenger lists, including around the time she married Leslie Wrigley in Australia in 1908. Uncle Les was born in Australia in 1876 and had a career in education. He graduated with honours from the University of Melbourne and later studied at the London Day Training College, which is possibly how he and Florence met. After returning to Australia he worked in a number of institutions and implemented teacher training courses. Later, he became professor and dean of education of Melbourne Teachers' College. An online biography describes him as a man with 'alarmingly rapid speech' and that his 'wiry frame embodied energy and a tremendous capacity for work ... his rimless pince-nez enhanced his reserved, scholarly appearance'.

Flo and Les would have visits from her family in England and these relatives appear in passenger lists sailing to Australia, including Walter (who received the postcard) and his family.

During a visit to England in 1932, Les was involved in a serious car accident and the couple stayed in the UK for an extended period while he recuperated, before returning to Australia with Flo's sister Agnes the following year. Les' health never fully recovered and he died in Australia a few months after their return.

RMS *Orsova* was owned by the Orient Line and you can read more about this company in the next postcard story – sent to a child of the then owner.

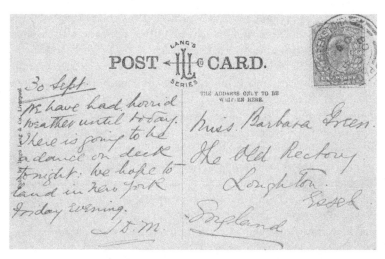

S033

Embarkation on Landing Stage, Liverpool

We have had horrid weather until today. There is going to be a dance on deck tonight. We hope to land in New York Friday evening.
JDM

I often say how surprised I am about where a postcard takes me and this one dropped me into the centre of British aristocracy and a story that requires a deep breath and a lot of concentration! Barbara's father was Sir Frederick Green. Born in 1871, he was a member of the family that ran the Orient Line – a shipping company that began trading in the late 18th century. It would eventually become part of P&O with that company owning a majority share in 1919 that ultimately led to it being absorbed into the parent company. Barbara's grandfather, also named Frederick and knighted, married Alice Cooper, daughter of politician Sir Daniel Cooper. Sir Daniel spent much of his life and career in Australia, where Alice was born.

Barbara's mother, Cicely Maitland, was the daughter of John Maitland, rector of Loughton and 'lord of the manor'. Cicely's mother, Venetia, was the daughter of Sir Richard Digby Neave – author, artist and director of several railway companies. More than one biography mentions that he was a friend of artist John Constable. His brother, Sheffield Neave, became governor of the Bank of England in 1857.

Barbara's brother, John Green, married Margaret Holford in 1923. Margaret was the daughter of James Holford and Blanche née Grosvenor, daughter of Richard Grosvenor, 1st Baron Stalbridge, a politician, and son of the 2nd Marquess of Westminster.

As I reached further into Barbara's extended family, almost every connection revealed a story that linked to some of the most famous families in the UK. Even John Green's probate records include a baron – Baron Bicester. Sir Lancelot Royle is also mentioned. He participated in the 1924 '*Chariots of Fire*' Olympics as a sprinter, winning gold in the relay.

And what of Barbara? In 1920 she married William Mitford. In the 1911 census, William's father, William Kenyon Mitford, is recorded as 'colonel royal bodyguard'. After serving in the army, including service abroad in the Boer War, he was aide-de-camp for yeomanry to Kings Edward VII and George V. The family lived at Pitshill House in Sussex – the house was built (although not completed) in 1760 by the Mitford family. William Kenyon Mitford was the son of the Conservative MP for Sussex, William Townley

Mitford. His mother, Margaret née Kenyon, was daughter of the 3rd Baron Kenyon, whose family's history also includes MPs.

It seems likely that the postcard was sent by passengers of SS *Lucania*, based on the date on the card and the expected arrival in New York. Perhaps, given the initials, they were Barbara's relatives from the Maitland branch.

S027

Mother.

*Although there's no address or anything else on the reverse of the card,
I do hope Mother received her card.*

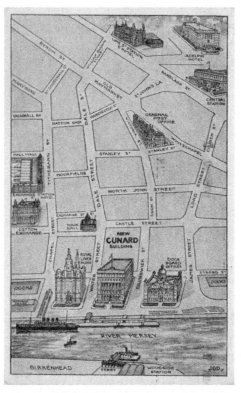

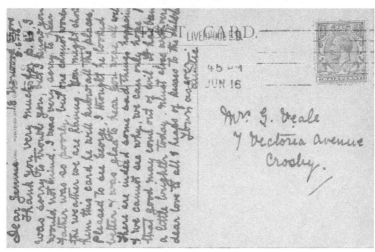

S052

New Cunard Building and River Mersey

48

8 June 1916
Mrs G Veale
7 Victoria Avenue
Crosby

Dear Jennie
Thank you very much for PC.
I was sorry to trouble you, but I know you would not mind.
I was very sorry to hear Father was so poorly, but one cannot wonder the weather we are
having. You might show him this card he will know all the places. Pleased to see George,
I thought he looked better, and was glad to hear you were all well. There are indeed some
bad things happening and we cannot see why, we can only hope that good may come out of
evil. It has been a little brighter today.
Must close with very dear love to all and heaps of kisses to the children.
Yours as ever.
Auntie

Jane Wilson was writing to her niece, Jennie née Wilson, from her home in
Norwood Grove, Liverpool where she lived with another niece, Sophia.
Jennie had married George Veale in 1899 – he was the son of sea captain
Isaac Veale, who would certainly have been familiar with Liverpool's docks
and the surrounding area. As would George, a shipping clerk working for a
steamship company. Jennie's father, Henry Wilson, had a career with the
railways and at the time Jennie married he was the local manager of the
Lancashire and Yorkshire Railway. However, he too had connections with
the sea – his father was a captain.

The timing of the postcard suggests that Jane was referring to the vicious
fighting in France – it would only be a few weeks before the slaughter of the
Battle of the Somme began.

S018

Arrival of Steamers, Douglas, Isle of Man

16 September 1908
Mrs Swingler
81 Nidd Road
Off Staniforth Road
Attercliffe
[Sheffield]

Esplanade, Central Promenade, Douglas

Dear Sister
Just a line, we are having awful weather. It is that rough you cannot keep on your feet.
Rained every day since we came. I hope to goodness it will be a bit better before we come
back so that we can get out a bit. We were nearly tossed off the boat coming. We were
sticking like glue. We shall have to wait until it is better before we come back or I think
we shall be washed overboard. It is raining down now, never ceased today.
Write back when you get this.
With love Lizzie

Elizabeth Bennett, known as Lizzie, was writing to her sister, Evelyn, who
had married John Swingler in 1904. He worked as a boiler fireman with a
steel manufacturer. In 1911, Lizzie lived with her parents – her father, Henry
Bennett, also worked for a steel manufacturer, as a looker-over of steel. By
this time, Lizzie was almost 40 and no employment is recorded.

As amusing as Lizzie's message is to read now, the journey does sound
awful – especially when it's likely she wasn't necessarily able to take too many
holidays away from home.

S085

SS Montrose

Mrs P Bridson
Portaballa
Ballasalla
Isle of Man

Dear Ellen
We have arrived in Liverpool all safe. We had a splendid passage. The children ran about all the voyage. We were not a bit seasick. Met Dick and Emma. Hoping it will be fine tomorrow.
CB

Once I had traced the Bridson family to Ballasalla I soon discovered that the postcard was sent between sisters – Christian and Eleanor née Quayle. Eleanor, who received the postcard, married Paul Bridson in 1891 and Christian married Paul's cousin, Thomas Bridson, in 1895.

Canadian records show that Christian, Thomas and their children first left the Isle of Man for Canada in 1907. The postcard was sent when the couple and their children returned to Canada after a visit home three years later. In many of the families I've researched that involve emigration from the UK, especially to Canada, there are instances where they returned for visits. Sometimes these trips tied in with a bereavement, but more often they seemed to be returning for more pleasant reasons.

Christian and Thomas had five children that were born before they emigrated. Another daughter was born in Canada. Over the decades that followed, some of the children appear, as adults, in passenger lists; they clearly kept in touch with their roots in the Isle of Man.

The family arrived in Canada aboard SS *Montrose* on 4 May 1910. When I was deciding which postcards to include in this book, I was reminded of the story of Dr Crippen – the American physician who was found guilty of murdering his second wife, Cora, in London and then absconded with his lover. In 1910, Crippen and Ethel Le Neve sailed on *Montrose* from Belgium on their way across the Atlantic.

Despite the insistence of Miriam Williams (also known as Kate Roberts and weightlifting performer, Vulcana), who was a friend of Cora Turner's (also known as Corinne Mackamotzki and entertainer, Belle Elmore), that Cora had been murdered, the police were unable to find any evidence that Crippen had murdered his wife and that she had, as Crippen insisted, returned home to America. It was only because Crippen panicked and decided to flee London that the police's interest was piqued and his home searched more thoroughly – leading to the discovery of human remains in the basement which were eventually identified as Cora's.

Passenger lists show the main players in this story through the various episodes – Crippen and Le Neve are included as Mr and Master Robinson with Le Neve disguised as a boy aboard *Montrose*. It was her femininity that made Captain Kendall and the crew suspicious. She was a pretty woman and it's hard to imagine anyone believing her to be a boy. Her table manners drew attention before there was any suggestion that she was involved with Crippen and it's possible that if they had booked themselves a lower class of passage, they would have been lost within the crowded dining rooms.

As the pair had absconded, images of them circulated. Crippen's bushy moustache would make him recognisable. Captain Kendall is reported to have used white chalk to erase the moustache on the image he received. This clearly revealed who the Robinsons really were and a telegraph message, the first of its kind to apprehend a criminal, was sent:

Have strong suspicions that Crippen London cellar murderer and accomplice are among saloon passengers. Moustache taken off growing beard. Accomplice dressed as boy. Manner and build undoubtedly a girl.

Inspector Walter Dew – in charge of the case – sailed across the Atlantic on a faster ship, RMS *Laurentic*. Boarding *Montrose* disguised as a pilot, he arrested the couple and they returned to England on RMS *Megantic* and appear in the ship's passenger lists with Inspector Dew and various other security staff.

As fascinating as it is to see those passenger lists, I was also intrigued by how often Crippen crossed the Atlantic.

While still married to his first wife Charlotte, he sailed on SS *Amsterdam*. Later, after his wife's death, he crossed the Atlantic multiple times, perhaps visiting his son who was cared for by Crippen's parents. Over the years that followed, he appears in passenger lists for many of the ships you will find in this book – although none of the passengers I have researched shared their time with Crippen. However, the Bridson family sailed on *Montrose* with Captain Kendall at the helm shortly before Crippen's journey.

If you've read my first book, you will remember Captain Kendall from the tragic story of RMS *Empress of Ireland*. The ship regularly crossed the Atlantic from Liverpool to Quebec as part of the Canadian Pacific Line. Returning to England in 1914, the ship collided with another in the fog-bound St Lawrence River. Within 15 minutes of the collision, the ship sank and more than a thousand people lost their lives – including Edith Stainer from Dorchester who I'd researched through a postcard she sent to a cousin in Dorset. Captain Kendall was a reluctant survivor; hauled to safety he would suffer from survivor's guilt. More passengers lost their lives in this tragedy than in RMS *Titanic*'s – although overall, *Titanic*'s losses were greater. Despite those losses, the tragedy has been widely forgotten – overshadowed by the outbreak of the First World War and statistically coming second to *Titanic*. In Canada there are annual services of remembrance for those lost on the *Empress of Ireland*, including those held by the Salvation Army. More than 170 members and their families were travelling from Canada to an international congress at the Royal Albert Hall; all the adults were lost. Today, some recall seeing as children, first class cushions and lifebelts that had been washed ashore. They had been retrieved and kept in sheds and shown to curious children, before eventually being passed to a museum. For many years divers plundered the wreck of the ship but it is now protected and respected as a maritime grave.

Understandably Captain Kendall was reluctant to talk about the tragedy. In the last weeks of his life, his carers said that he often thrashed about, resisting help; his grandson believed he was reliving the moment he was dragged to safety.

Before Christian and Thomas left the Isle of Man for Canada, Thomas worked as a labourer. The Canadian census returns show that he was also a labourer in Ontario and that a daughter, May, was a mail clerk. Thomas junior was a gardener before he served in the First World War and was a labourer at the time of his marriage in 1923.

S068

SS Lake Champlain

1 March 1911
Miss JW Ballantine
Victoria Cottage
Caputh
Murthy
[Scotland]

Liverpool
After being on board with Bertie he is off and out of sight quite well and happy glad to say.
Now on way for ?

At talks, I'm sometimes asked at what stage I stop my research. When I'm working on a card that reveals very little – in the case of this one – I often wonder if I'm just 'one click away' from a discovery. Fortunately, in this case, going for that extra click revealed a fascinating story.

According to the 1901 census, James Ballantine was an insurance agent (other records show he worked on an estate). He lived in Victoria Cottage with his wife, son and three daughters. That is their story. What would one more click reveal?

Often I like to see if the homes lived in are still there and Victoria Cottage is now holiday accommodation and renamed as Miss Ballantine's Cottage, in honour of James' youngest daughter, Georgina, who died there in the 1970s.

Georgina was a nurse during the First World War and was honoured for her work. However, she also has another claim to fame. In 1922 she landed the biggest ever rod-caught salmon in Britain – on the River Tay that runs through the Glendelvine Estate in which Victoria Cottage stands. The 64-pound fish took more than two hours to land. Her father had rowed their small boat, supporting Georgina as she fought the fish. It measured just under five feet in length – almost as long as Georgina was tall. After a cast was taken, the fish was donated to Perth Royal Infirmary. Georgina's record was celebrated around the country with the record making newspaper headlines. The incredible achievement was commemorated in a watercolour painting by AJ Rennie which was hung in a London gentlemen's club. It might seem strange to us today, but despite the gents wanting to celebrate Georgina's success, she wasn't permitted into the club to see the painting hung.

I was unable to trace Bertie – his ship's passenger lists have several candidates but without something more than a possible connection to Scotland, I wasn't able to find him.

S058

Queenstown

23 August 1920
Miss L Croucher
Westport House
Reigate
England

Dear Miss Croucher
Just to wish you many happy returns of the day, hoping you are having a good time. It is
simply gorgeous here and the weather is not too bad.
BKW

Lillian Croucher was the daughter of Elizabeth Parker and Charles Croucher. When the couple married in 1891, Elizabeth's address is given as Leith Villa, Reigate – with no occupation. However, a few months earlier, the census return shows her there as a cook working for Lord Richard Browne – a retired major who was born in Jamaica. Baptism and probate records mention that he was 'commonly called' Lord but he hasn't included the title in the 1911 census. In earlier records he is listed as Lord Browne and his wife as Agnes, Lady Browne.

Richard's father was the 2nd Marquess of Sligo, Howe Browne, who was born in Westport House, County Mayo. As a young man, Howe was a traveller and enjoyed trips to Greece with his friend, Lord Byron. Prime Minister Robert Peel, a school friend, appointed Howe governor of Jamaica in 1834 where he was to implement the Slavery Abolition Act of 1833. His initiatives included the opening of schools (two of which he financed) and an apprentice system for freed slaves. However, this scheme is now widely regarded as slavery in all but name. Still, in Jamaica, the first free slave village was renamed Sligoville in his honour. Many of his peers viewed him as a traitor and his character was attacked in newspapers both in Jamaica and in the UK. Eventually he was forced to leave before his work was finished. The family's ancestral home in County Mayo is now dedicated to the memory of Howe Browne's work in the abolition of slavery.

To many, Howe was a champion of the slaves. However, he was also a slave owner, inheriting two plantations in Jamaica – and the slave workers – from a grandmother. In the 1830s, he received almost £6,000 from the British government when his 286 slaves were freed. In all, £20 million was paid out as compensation to slave owners – the equivalent of £17 billion today – for the forced disposal of their 'assets'. You can learn more about slave owners and the compensation they received via the Centre for the Study of the Legacies of British Slavery's searchable database. You will find where the owners lived in the UK, how many slaves they owned and how much compensation they received. Many of us consider the slave owners to be vastly wealthy, owning estates both in the UK and the Caribbean. However, when you search the database for your own area, you might find a widow, a vicar owning one or two slaves that were 'leased' out to the plantation owners. It would be easy to assume we have no slave-owning ancestors, and hopefully that is the case, but the exploitation and cruelty could be nearer to your roots than you might think.

Despite that negative aspect, I found it touching that Elizabeth and Charles Croucher would have acknowledged her former employer's family history by naming their own home, Westport House.

When Lillian Croucher, who received the card, married farmer Dudley Beven at the age of 34 in 1927, her occupation is given as Political Organiser (Conservative). It's possible that she may have worked with the Primrose League – an organisation founded in 1883 that promoted the ideals of the Conservative Party. Lillian's sister, Gladys, worked in a similar capacity. However, by 1939 she is recorded as 'Political Organiser unemployed'.

S107

Moscow, 1912 – posted to Yorkshire

Have had a long day and are very tired.
Compliments and love from G & E Goddard.

S098

Hotel Metropole, Las Palmas

20 October 1908
H Greener Esq
6 Tyfica Crescent
Pontypridd
Beddau
South Wales

The Fire at this Hotel on August 28th only destroyed 36 bedrooms, the Hotel being reopened for business three days after, and has been well patronised since. The burnt rooms will be ready again for occupation by Xmas. The whole Hotel is likewise being redecorated and refurbished. A fine programme of entertainments has been arranged for the season, and especially for Xmas.
J. Sauerbrei
Manager

The manager of the Metropole in Las Palmas was keen to inform potential guests that the hotel was open for business and a good time was assured. We can assume the recipients of Mr Sauerbrei's cards were past visitors, but it wasn't possible to find Henry Greener in passenger lists to confirm this. By the time of the 1911 census, he and his wife, Jane, were at Beddau and Henry appears in an electoral register for 1908 at Tyfica Crescent.

Henry had worked as a colliery manager and was born in Wylam, Northumberland in 1838. In 1862 he married Jane Pearson and by 1911, only four of their 14 children were alive – that's a heartbreaking statistic.

Thirty-one-year-old Benjamin died in July 1908 – not long before the postcard was sent. He had worked in a colliery as a fireman and for more than seven years, suffered from a disease associated with tuberculosis.

Almost 20 years after Mr Sauerbrei's marketing drive, Agatha Christie left Southampton for Las Palmas aboard SS *Gelria* with her daughter and secretary, sailing to a warm place to write and relax. Agatha Christie stayed in the Canaries for three months, some of it spent at the Metropole, and later used it as the setting for *The Companion*, a Miss Marple story. She describes the Metropole as 'the principal hotel in Las Palmas' and the perfect location for swimming and surfing.

Agatha Christie included in her story a mention of Royal Holland Lloyd, the shipping line that owned *Gelria*. Nine hundred of the passengers sailed in steerage and the remaining 600 were split between first, second and third class. Also on board with Agatha Christie – heading for Brazil, the ship's ultimate destination – was Lilian Elliott a writer who worked for *The Times*. In 1919, she had become their South American correspondent. As well as writing for the newspaper, she also wrote books, including a novel, *Black Gold*.

SANTA CRUZ DE TENERIFE.   GENERAL VIEW.

I was sorry I could not get this posted at Teneriffe. No one went on shore. I will write our address again, I doubt whether it is very distinct in my lette. — Hotel Metropole, Las Palmas, Grand Canary. —

UNIÓN POSTAL UNIVERSAL
UNION POSTALE UNIVERSELLE
ESPAÑA

A Miss E. P. Thompson
Beaconfield Lodge
Lansdown
Bath
England

En este lado se escribe solamente la dirección.

S097

Santa Cruz, Tenerife

64

2 April 1904
Miss EP Thompson
Beaconfield Lodge
Lansdown
Bath
England

I was sorry I could not get this posted at Tenerife. No one went ashore. I will write our
address again. I doubt whether it is very ... in my letter.
Hotel Metropole, Las Palmas, Grand Canary.

Authors and sisters Ellen Perronet and Edith Thompson were born in Kent and had moved to Bath from Surrey with their parents. Their father, Thomas, was a county court judge.

As an author, Ellen's work was often credited to E Perronet Thompson and she was sometimes referred to as Elizabeth, but she was actually named after her mother, Ellen James, who was born in France.

When Edith died in 1929 at the age of 80, her obituary mentions that she was 'notable in the literary world'.

Edith provided most of the 15,000 quotations for the first edition of the *Oxford English Dictionary*, that are credited to the sisters, and she edited and proofread several large sections. The sisters would have been children when work was first began (by others) on the dictionary in 1857. Its first section was published almost 30 years later and the work would continue into the 1920s. Edith also wrote *History of England* which was used as part of the 'Historical Course for Schools' and acted as consultant for historical terms used in the dictionary.

When novelist Pip Williams wrote her book, *The Dictionary of Lost Words*, she wanted to honour the sisters' work, especially Edith's immense contribution, and included a fictionalised version of her within the novel's plot. Edith appears as Aunt Ditte, godmother to the fictional Esme. According to the plot, Aunt Ditte worked on the dictionary from her home in Bath, which she shared with a sister (Ellen), and had written a history of England. Esme's widowed father is a fictional character, but the plot describes a team of lexicographers working at Sunnyside, in Oxford – the real home of James Murray, who was tasked by the Philological Society of England to head the team who would research the words of the English language.

The sisters' grandfather, Thomas Perronet Thompson, was governor of Sierra Leone and known as a radical reformer. He wrote *The True Theory of Rent* and *A Catechism on the Corn Laws*. An uncle, Lieutenant Colonel John Thompson, served in the Crimean War.

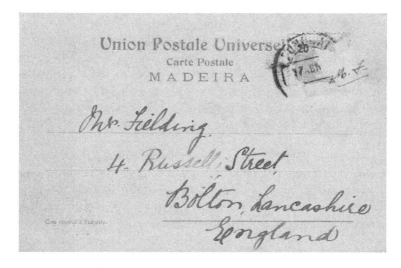

S103

Reid's Palace Hotel, Madeira

Mrs Fielding
4 Russell Street
Bolton
Lancashire
England

We are staying here. How is Harold, as have only heard once from him since he left Canary,
but hope he is well & you all at home.
Kind remembrances
May P

It's not possible to know if May was actually staying in the hotel depicted on the card – but what a wonderful experience it would have been if she had. The hotel opened in the early 1890s and later provided a 'luxury retreat combining Edwardian elegance with the latest comforts of the day'. Guests included politicians Winston Churchill, Anthony Eden and David Lloyd George. Later, film stars Roger Moore and Gregory Peck would also stay there.

All that luxury would come at a price, but May's party were clearly enjoying a wonderful holiday that included the Canary Islands.

Harold Fielding, mentioned in the message, was born in Lancashire in 1880 and married Alice Sharman, the daughter of brewer and pub owner Joseph Sharman, in February 1909. A month earlier, his name appears in passenger lists, returning from Las Palmas to Liverpool.

Harold was a clerk and later became a manager in a cotton factory, which ties in very nicely with his father's work. John Fielding was born in Blackburn in 1849 and began work at the age of 12 in a mill, possibly with *his* father. In 1874, he was appointed secretary to the Bolton Trades' Council and later to the Operative Spinners' Provincial Association, a trade union. John died when Harold was only 14. He was a well-respected man and a statue was erected in Queen's Park, Bolton in his memory. The inscription reads:

JT Fielding, JP
For over 20 years the secretary of the Operative Cotton Spinners' Association and United Trades Council of Bolton and District. Unity and Equity were the guiding principles of his life. Erected by the Trade Unionists and Public of Bolton and presented to the Borough July 11 1896 [two years after his death at the age of 45].

Frances née Guffogg, who received the card, was the daughter of a mangler who worked in a cotton factory. At the time Frances married John Fielding, she worked in the same industry. The next generation, her daughters – Harold's sisters – worked in offices and as teachers (Emily would become a headteacher).

S083

RMS *Adriatic*

13 April 1916
Miss EP Hogan
Box 308
Amherst NS

Dear EP
At last we are on board. We are still out in the harbour. There's a mail going ashore in a few minutes. Everything is OK. Classy state rooms and dining rooms. Some ship. This is her on other side. Will write you on the way over.

Exact dates vary as to when RMS *Adriatic* began its First World War duties transporting troops across the Atlantic, but she was certainly in service around the time this postcard was written.

The website Wartime Canada includes a booklet produced for a sailing a few weeks later, listing all the crew and 'passengers' including a naval officer, Assistant Paymaster Hogan. Another website says that *Adriatic* didn't serve under the Liner Requisition Scheme (carrying troops and ammunition) until the following year.

Edna Hogan was born in Nova Scotia in 1894. Her parents, James Hogan and Martha née Peart, had at least 12 children and Edna was the eldest.

Two of her brothers served in the First World War – although I couldn't find a close relative who might have been Assistant Paymaster Hogan.

Robert and Charles were bank clerks. Robert's attestation paper, dated 1915 when he was 18, gives the same address as that on the postcard. Unfortunately, neither brothers' handwriting matches that on the card.

In 1921, Edna married Harold Pickard. He was also a bank clerk who served in the war – but again, his handwriting isn't a match.

Edna's youngest brother, Joseph (Joe), wasn't born until 1919 and he enlisted for service during the Second World War in the Royal Canadian Airforce. In 1943, following a raid on Mannheim in Germany his aircraft was brought down and crashed onto the roof of the Grands Magasins du Louvre department store in the centre of Paris. The Canadian Royal Airforce and other Second World War sites provide more information: *An Avro Lancaster from the No. 57 Squadron RAF, based at RAF East Kirkby, was hit by German flak and crashed into the building on the night of 23 September 1943, almost completely destroying the interior, leaving only the exterior walls standing. The Canadian pilot, Joe Douglas Hogan and six crew members were all killed.* Joe and the other members of the crew – from Canada, England and Australia – were buried in France.

S084

RMS Laurentic

7 April 1911
Mrs Allen
'Arundle'
Alton Park Road
Clacton-on-Sea
Essex

Liverpool
Dear Mother
Arrived L safely. Only stopped at Edge Hill and Crewe.
Have got in good hotel and cheap and have found a friend.
He is a Irishman so we have just gone and booked our berths in same cabin.
I shall meet a Welshman tonight.
I will send you a card from Queenstown.
Have looked round Liverpool it is a large place.
I had to fill up another form at offices as the other one went with the other boat.
With love from Horace

There's something of a sense of adventure in this card's message. Horace was leaving England, making jokes and on his way to America. Why was he catching a different boat?

Interestingly, he appears in the passenger lists for RMS *Laurentic*, which sailed from Liverpool on 11 March 1911, arriving nine days later – before the date on the postcard. That record shows that Horace's intended destination was Rocky River, Ohio. There's also a description of his appearance: 5'8" tall, brown hair, hazel eyes and a light complexion. He had $19 with him. Those details were crossed out – confirming Horace didn't sail at that time. This is also verified by the postcard's date and his inclusion in the 1911 census – taken on 2 April. On 8 April, Horace finally sailed to America aboard *Laurentic*. In the intervening days, his funds were reduced to only $17.

Four years later, in May 1915, he returned to England aboard SS *Orduña* and a month later, he enlisted in the army and served in the First World War. A brother, Raymond, was killed in 1918 and is buried in Belgium. He had enlisted, at the age of 18, the previous year.

Horace wasn't the only member of his family to live abroad. His mother Emily's brother, Edwin Gibbens, eventually settled in Canada. When he married in 1918, at the age of 41, he was a farmer. His wife, Mary Halligan, was a clerk from Ireland. Some records suggest Mary wasn't his first wife, although he married in Canada as a bachelor.

Horace was one of nine children, some of whom were born in areas now regarded as in or near to London – Hammersmith, Hatford and Watford. Other siblings were born further afield: Kingston-on-Thames, Bexhill, Raynes Park and even Worthing. Horace's parents, Ernest Allen and Emily

Gibbens, were born in Walworth (London) and Abingdon, Berkshire. There's nothing in the family's tree to suggest why they moved around so much – Ernest was a draper's assistant and, later, a tailor.

Horace died just a few weeks before his one hundredth birthday.

S095

Paris – posted to Australia in 1911

With love from the top!

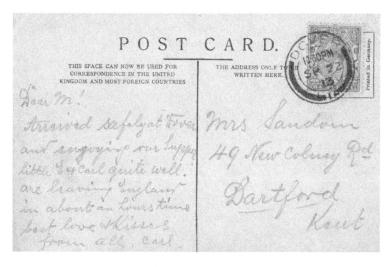

S063

Dover from the Western Heights

22 September 1913
Mrs Sandom
49 New Colney Road
Dartford, Kent

Dear M!
Arrived safely at Dover and enjoying our supper. Little E and Carl quite well. Are leaving
England in about an hour's time.
Best love and kisses from all.
Carl

Grocer Carl Wagner sent the postcard to his mother-in-law, Emma. He was leaving on a trip with his wife, Emma, and their two young children, Johannes Carl and Emma. Carl and Emma had married in 1908, and in 1910, Carl is included in a directory at 67 Fulwell Road, Teddington. Although this is a residential road, number 67 was a commercial property – as it is today – with a flat on the first floor. In 1911, it was occupied by a family running a general store. But in the 1911 census, Emma appears with her and Carl's children, living with her mother at the address on the card.

Emma Warren married Daniel Sandom in 1882. Daniel was a blacksmith and their son, Harold, became a mill shop foreman. Before their marriage, Emma appears in records working as a maid for manufacturing silversmith, Stephen Smith.

Smith had continued his father's business, and eventually his own son, Stephen junior, would work with him. The business thrived and they had premises within sight of London's Covent Garden. They were there 30 or so years after the covered market that we recognise today was built. Later, the business traded in Oxford Street and was eventually sold to Mappin & Webb. There are many examples of beautiful Stephen Smith silverware online – they come with a hefty price tag!

While it's lovely to see family names being repeated through the generations, three generations of Emmas must have caused some confusion at times. I have this in my own family, where my father and grandfather shared the same first name. To avoid confusion, they always called Dad by his middle name.

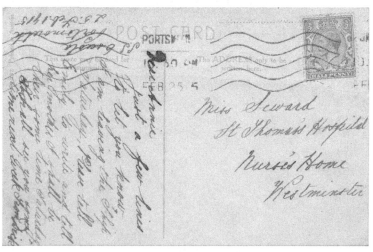

S040

25 February 1915
Miss Seward
St Thomas's Hospital
Nurses' Home
Westminster

Dear Annie
Just a few lines to let you know I am leaving the ship Saturday. Please tell Emily to write
and tell her mother I shall be there some time Saturday. I shall see you some time next
week. From Dick.

Although there's no record of Annie Seward working as a nurse in St
Thomas's hospital, she appears in the 1911 census with her father, Herbin
(Herbert), and six siblings living within the hospital where he was an
engineer's labourer.

The London Metropolitan Archives confirms that during the early years
of the 20th century, there were a significant number of improvements to the
hospital, 'including the introduction of electric lighting … in both theatres
and wards'. It's no surprise, therefore, to see that also living on the hospital's
site were electricians Arthur Branch and William Crooke and their wives and
children.

Annie's youngest sister, Elizabeth, was only one year old when their
mother, Annie née Dening, died. The accommodation offered by the hospital
would have been basic, but it was a place where Herbin would be able to care
for the children – with Annie's help. She was born in 1892, so a great
responsibility rested with her. Aged 16, Herbin junior worked as a labourer
with a mechanic but later he would also work in a hospital – as an engineer
of hot water steam heating.

Elizabeth, the youngest sibling, married valet Ralph Blackwell in 1935. He
appears in the passenger lists for RMS *Mauretania* in 1928, sailing to New
York, returning a few weeks later aboard SS *Aquitania*. In 1939 he was butler
and valet to Privy Councillor Oliver Stanley. The following year, the politician
was appointed Secretary of State for War – the same role held by his father
during the First World War. However, after only a few months he was
replaced by Anthony Eden.

Annie married seaman Albert Ladbrook in 1920. Perhaps he is the
connection with the postcard – but the handwriting doesn't match his
signature in the marriage register. In fact, where it was possible to check her
brothers' writing, none were a match for Dick's and I couldn't find Emily.
By 1939, Albert had left the sea and was working as a labourer in St Thomas's
Hospital – although the couple lived in Wandsworth. Annie's brother,
Ernest, was also connected with the sea, as a sailor. He died, aged just 19, of
bronchial pneumonia while serving on HMS *Sunflower* in 1919.

The Quays, (Bangor Steamer).   Belfast.

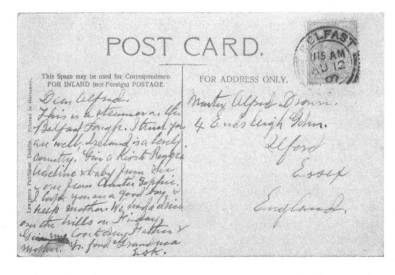

S082

The Quays, Belfast

12 August 1907
Master Alfred Drown
4 Endsleigh Gardens
Ilford
Essex
England

Dear Alfred
This is a steamer on the Belfast Lough. I trust you are well. Ireland is a lovely country.
Give a kiss to Reggie Adeline and baby from me and one from Auntie Sophie. I hope you
are a good boy and help Mother. We had a drive over the hills on Friday. Give my love to
your father and mother. Your fond Grandma.
ESK

Emma Sophie Kolkenbeck was visiting Ireland with her youngest daughter, Sophie, who was born in 1873. Emma was the daughter of Paul Munster, Danish Consul for Ireland – where she was born. Emma married Hermann Kolkenbeck in 1861 in Ireland. More than 25 years later, Hermann, who was born in Germany, became a naturalised British citizen and worked as a commercial clerk in London. With Emma, he had at least six children – including Mary, Alfred's mother. Although Mary was born in London, her siblings were born in other countries, including Russia. Her brother Alfred was born in Belgium and became a translator and export merchant.

Alfred, who received the card, was one of at least six children born to Mary and William Drown. William was from Devon and his father was a blacksmith and engineer with the Royal Navy. William was a metallurgist and worked for the Royal Mint during the First World War. His obituary mentions that he was *in direct charge of ... ingot stock of gold ... It was under his control of the Royal Mint operative department that all coinages and medals were struck during the war.*

Alfred became an accountant and one of his sisters, Norah, became a doctor and worked at the Jenny Lind Hospital which cared for children in Norwich. The hospital opened in the 1850s and was named after the Swedish singer who supported the hospital and others around the country.

S004

RMS Royal George

29 March 1911
Miss Clayton
14 Hebron Road
Hammersmith
London
England

Dear N
I thought you would like a postcard of the boat I came out with, it's very nice but it does roll. If ever you want to see a rough sea go to the Picture Palace not on board.
Cliff

Builder Cliff Clayton's stay in Canada wasn't a long one – he returned to England as a married man aboard RMS *Empress of Ireland* the following year. His wife, Hazel née Browne, was born in Canada but her English parents had returned home and lived in Islington, London. According to the passenger lists for RMS *Corsican*, Hazel sailed back to Canada in August 1911 'to be married' – which happened two months later in Winnipeg.

Ellen Clayton, who received the postcard, was Cliff's eldest sister. She was born in 1864, and in 1911 was still living with her parents, George and Mary. George had been a carpenter and a builder.

Like many of the ships featured in this collection, RMS *Royal George* was used during the First World War as a troop ship. In 1919 she was returned to Cunard who had bought all the Canadian Northern Steamships three years earlier. She continued to cross the Atlantic to Canada and America until 1920.

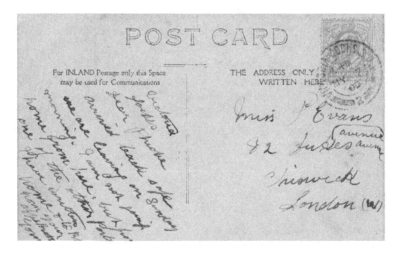

S002

7 May 1909
Miss P Evans
82 Duke's Avenue
Chiswick
London (W)

Victoria Docks
Dear Phoebe
Arrived back safe. We are leaving on Sunday morning. I am not going home from here,
but from one of the other ports. I have written home and to Bhm [Birmingham].
From your affectionate brother John.

Phoebe Evans was born in Fernhill Heath, Worcestershire in 1881. At the time the postcard was sent, she was working in Chiswick as a cook for Annie Gribble. She was one of at least nine children born to George and Francis/Fanny née Wilde – including John Wilde Evans who sent the postcard.

In later years, Phoebe would return to Worcestershire where she became an agricultural worker in Evesham. She appears in the 1939 register with her widowed father, who was at this time a retired agricultural worker.

Although Phoebe's mother, Fanny, was also born in Worcestershire, she appears in a census return before her marriage working for a family in Harrow, Middlesex as a nurse. Could this explain why Phoebe moved away from Worcestershire for a number of years? Had the family made contacts in the area?

John emigrated to Canada with a brother, Samuel, and it seems this postcard was sent on a visit home. They possibly made several return visits because in 1913, the brothers returned to Canada aboard RMS *Empress of Ireland*. Both brothers served in the First World War with the Canadian army. Samuel was killed in 1916 and John in 1917; both are buried in France. Before the war, the brothers lived together and worked on a farm in Ontario.

It's impossible to know if John appears in the postcard's photo – it would have been so useful if he had mentioned the image in his message. Also, it's unclear if Samuel is with him – although nothing in the message suggests his brother is on the ship.

S008

RMS Carmania

26 February
Miss A Miller
#13 Frances Street
Ashton-on-Ribble
Preston

Dear Ada
Just a line to let you see I am still alive. We have not been sick very much but we are having it very rough just now. We are on the banks of Newfoundland. It isn't half rocking. We are not expected to arrive till Monday morning. That is 12 days and is getting monotonous. From Ada

There were several passengers aboard RMS *Carmania* in February 1920 with the first name Ada. The ship arrived in New York on 1 March and after a process of elimination, one possible contender was Ada Banks who was born in Wiltshire in 1882 as Ada Pontin. She was travelling with her son, William, who was 15. Searching through the UK records led me to the family living in Wiltshire, Wales and Lancashire – and not far from Ada who received the card. William was born in Tyldesley which isn't far from Ashton-on-Ribble, but that doesn't prove a connection. Ada's husband, William Banks, declared on his naturalisation records in 1926 that he had arrived in America on RMS *Victorian* in 1919.

Ada Miller, who received the postcard, was one of ten children born to James and Annie. Like some of her sisters, Ada worked as a cotton weaver. In Detroit, Ada Banks also worked in a factory, William was a pipe fitter and their son became a die maker. But was this the Ada who sent the card?

These adventurous people who sailed across the Atlantic were in search of something they felt couldn't be found at home. Was working in a factory in Detroit any better than similar work in Lancashire?

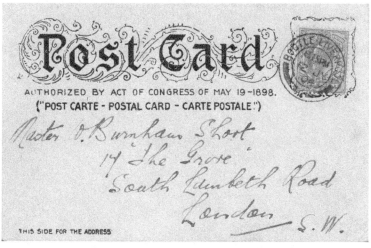

S046

Statue of Liberty, New York

12 July 1904
Master W Burnham Short
17 The Grove
South Lambeth Road
London SW

Hope your mother is better. Send me word. AB

William Burnham Short was born in 1894. His father, William senior, was a police constable who would marry three times. His first wife, Harriet Burnham, was William's mother.

A postcard sent from Liverpool with an image of the Statue of Liberty suggested to me that the sender, AB, might have been on their way across the Atlantic. Could there be a Burnham in passenger lists around this time?

I actually found Arthur Shout Burnham in the 1911 census, living in Birkenhead. Fortunately, as head of the household he had completed the return and his handwriting matched that on the card. At the time of the census, he was 42 years old and his occupation was given as 'own means'. In earlier records he is a shipping clerk – and that possibly explains how he came by this postcard. Although working as a clerk was definitely an improvement on manual work, in reality the clerks were still paid a relatively low wage. However, it does seem that Arthur's status was financially secure and perhaps he even had a managerial role that eventually led to him living on his 'own means' by 1911.

Twenty years earlier he was living with his maternal grandfather, William Shout, in Boston, Lincolnshire. William was a registrar of births and deaths and in earlier records a solicitor's managing clerk and collector of water rates.

Young William, who received the card from his uncle, served in the Royal Navy during the First World War. On enlisting he was a motor mechanic and his naval records show that he was over six feet tall, had brown hair and grey eyes. In later years he became a driver for the Imperial Tobacco Company.

Harriet, William's mother and Arthur's sister, died in 1911 – years after her health was worrying Arthur.

The mixture of Shout and Short in this family's tree was fun to unravel – the handwriting in some of the records could have added to any confusion. It's always worthwhile looking at the maternal lines further back because they often reveal a family name used for later generations.

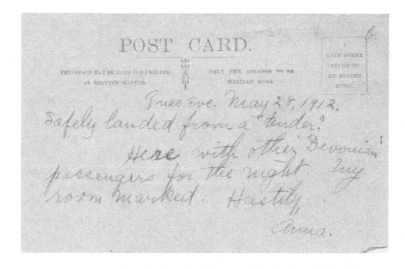

S056

North Western Hotel, Lime Street Station, Liverpool

28 May 1912
Tuesday evening
Safely landed from a 'tender'.
Here with other 'Devonian' passengers for the night. My room marked.
Hastily
Anna

Although Anna's postcard didn't have a recipient's address, with the name of the ship and the date she arrived in Liverpool, it was possible to confirm that Anna was Anna Pope and that she had sailed from Boston, Massachusetts. The passenger lists show she was employed as a secretary with the YWCA. She had applied for a passport in May 1912 and had then declared that she would be returning to America in September (she returned aboard SS *Winifredian*). That application described her as being 5'4" tall, having very dark brown eyes, a low forehead, a pointed nose with a dent, a slight double chin, slightly greying black hair and a mouth that was not full. The application didn't include a photograph – but the description is as unflattering as most of our passport photographs tend to be.

Anna was born in Spencer, Massachusetts in 1877. Her father, Joseph, was a grocer. A year after her visit to England, Anna married Edward Kelly, a minister and teacher.

In 1917, SS *Devonian* was sunk by a German U-boat off the north-east coast of Ireland. *Winifredian* was also involved in the First World War as a troop carrier, but before this she helped to return officers to England from Cape Town following the end of the Second Boer War.

Anna's hotel opened in 1871 and had 330 rooms. It closed in the 1930s and was owned for a while by John Moores University to be used as student accommodation. Later, it was sold again and restored as a hotel, albeit with a different name.

P.S. "KOH-I-NOOR" NEARING DOVER.

Published by The New Palace Steamers, Ltd.

S003

PS Koh-I-Noor

28 August 1909
Mrs J Vellensworth
The Lodge
Leith Park Road
Gravesend
Kent

Saturday
Dear Mother
Arrived safely. All well. Splendid trip. Met Alf Gee on boat. Hope you are better. With love.
Letter following.

John Vellensworth sent the postcard to his widowed mother, Eliza. Presumably he was on a trip with his wife, Ellen née Anthony, and perhaps their youngest child, Mary, who would have been almost ten at this time. John was a police inspector and it's possible to track his career through the census returns – beginning as a constable.

The Vellensworth family's story is a sad one – just a few months after the postcard, Ellen died. The following year, Eliza, who received the card, died – she had been a widow for almost 17 years. In November 1918, John's eldest son, Henry, was killed in France, fighting in the First World War. Almost exactly a year later, John died.

John's other son, Edward, worked as a clerk for the Port of London Authority. In 1939, his wife, Alice, ran a confectionery and tobacconist shop in The Terrace, Gravesend. Mary, John's youngest child, became a shorthand typist, working in a hotel in Southend-on-Sea, living with her Aunt Emma (John's sister).

Paddle Steamer *Koh-I-Noor* worked mainly along the Kent coast. She was removed from service at the outbreak of the First World War and eventually sent to Morecambe to be broken-up.

Although I found a family with the name Gee living relatively close to the Vellensworths, it would be impossible to confirm I had the right Mr Gee. William Gee was a lighterman (transporting goods to and from ships in a flat-bottomed barge) and was born in 1828. As he had at least nine sons (and four daughters), John could have met one of the sons, or one of the grandsons – although by 1909 many of the family members had moved away.

S092A

Liverpool Overhead Railway & St Nicholas' Church
Posted to London in 1908

S092B

St Nicholas' Church & New Tower Buildings, Liverpool
Posted to Bath in 1912

Many of the postcards I've researched begin their stories in Liverpool – from where passengers sailed across the Atlantic to either Canada or America. The city has been a port for centuries, beginning with trade across the Irish Sea. Later, the need for tobacco and sugar consignments extended the routes across the Atlantic and then to the Far East and Australia. By the 19th century, the docks had even become a tourist attraction. Today, following the decline of the shipping industry, those docks have been regenerated and are once again attracting visitors.

The building you see in the first postcard, to the right of the church of Saint Nicholas, is a signalling tower. As trade increased, an effective means of communication was needed to alert the docks to the arrival of ships. So, in 1824, an application was made to Parliament which resulted in the authorisation by the Liverpool Dock Trustees to *establish a speedy Mode of Communication to the Ship-owners and Merchants at Liverpool of the arrival of Ships and Vessels off the Port of Liverpool or the Coast of Wales, by building, erecting and maintaining Signal Houses, Telegraphs or such other Modes of Communication as to them shall seem expedient, between Liverpool and Hoylake, or between Liverpool and the Isle of Anglesey.* Over the years that followed the number of towers and their efficiency was improved – including the introduction of telegraphic messages. The smaller towers along the coast of North Wales had living accommodation, much like would be found for a lighthouse keeper – although the men were employed by the Board and not Trinity House.

The card was posted in 1908, just before the tower was demolished and replaced with the 'new' Tower Buildings – purpose-built office accommodation for businesses associated with the docks. The postcard of this new building was sent in 1912, not long after construction had been completed.

Many businesses and organisations had their offices there, including the Lloyds Register of British and Foreign Shipping and the American Consulate.

On the 6th floor, Joseph Chadwick had offices for a number of his businesses. The Chadwick family have long associations with shipping in Liverpool. Daniel Chadwick (Joseph's father) was born in the 1790s and ran a number of businesses connected with the trade, including rope-making – a big business in Liverpool and other towns and cities. HMS *Victory*, for example, needed 27 miles of rope for her rigging.

In the 1842 Commissioners' Report of Children's Employment, a Chadwick business is recorded as having *no steam machinery; there is some moveable machinery, drawn by horses … The regular hours are 6 to 6 … No bad language is used on the premises.*

The 1860 edition of *Gore's Directory of Liverpool*, shows that the Chadwick family's businesses had grown to include 'sail-making, chandlery, etc.', and could be found at several addresses near to the docks, including Bishopsgate Street where they had a large ropery which closed in the mid-1870s.

Joseph became Chairman of the Liverpool Ship Owners' Association and worked on other committees including the Mersey Docks and Harbour Board. His eldest son, Robert (born in 1869), continued the work into the next generation, and by this time the Chadwicks had become shipowners – ships that mainly carried cargo rather than passengers.

Robert worked in the Ministry of Munitions as Director of Overseas Transport during the First World War. As well as running the family business, Robert helped found the Honourable Company of Master Mariners. He was also a politician and was elected as MP for Wallasey in 1922 and was Parliamentary Secretary for the Board of Trade in Stanley Baldwin's government in the 1920s. In 1935 he was created 1st Baronet Chadwick of Bidston, Cheshire and changed his name by Deed Poll to Robert Burton-Chadwick.

Although the date of the advertisement on the next page isn't known, the business grew and merged with others and traded with different owners and names.

Robert was one of at least five siblings. A brother, Arthur, became a school teacher, working in the Isle of Man before opening his own school, Forres, in Northwood near Uxbridge. He was only 40 years old when he died in 1912 and the school was then run by his brother, Rohan, a vicar. Rohan moved Forres to Swanage, Dorset and one notable pupil there in the early years was the politician, Michael Foot.

Arthur had several children. His daughter, Cicely, married an architect. It's sometimes said that a person is 'ahead of their time' and this is certainly true of Cicely's husband, Valentine Harding. Looking at images of the houses he designed in the 1930s, it's hard to accept that they are now almost a hundred years old. Valentine served in the army during the Second World War and was killed at Dunkirk.

Another child of Arthur and his wife, Muriel, was Trevor. He would eventually teach at Forres in Swanage, but his family are recorded as thinking he was an underachiever at university. However, he certainly redeemed himself in the eyes of his family and the wider world.

Before the outbreak of the Second World War, Trevor was greatly affected by the plight of Jewish children in Prague. Reports of their persecution motivated him to work with a team of like-minded brave individuals who managed to help more than 10,000 children escape from Nazi-occupied territories via what is now known as Kindertransport – 669 children were rescued from Czechoslovakia (the Czech Republic). While some of the team worked in the UK, Trevor was based in Prague, putting himself at great risk as he helped as many children as possible leave for Britain.

In Prague, at the Wilson railway station (named, after the First World War, to honour American President Woodrow Wilson), a statue has been erected in memory of Sir Nicholas Winton – coordinator and saviour for so many of the children. Sir Nicholas was the son of German-Jewish parents and was educated at Stowe. Later, he would work abroad in Europe and was familiar with the restrictions placed on children travelling unaccompanied – it was his efforts in persuading Parliament to amend the law which ultimately enabled so many children to travel to safety. Trevor Chadwick was an important member of Sir Nicholas' team.

In the summer of 2022, Trevor's bravery was recognised by the unveiling of a statue in Swanage depicting him with two young children.

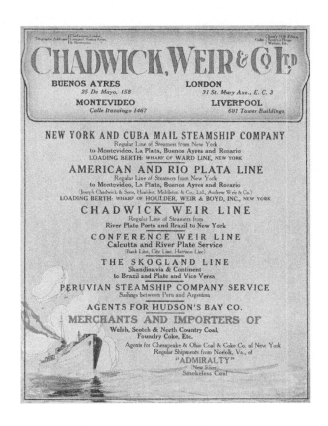

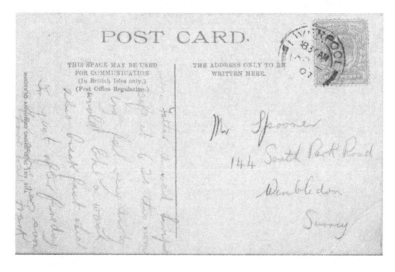

S009

S.S Tunisian

April 1907
Mr Spooner
144 South Park Road
Wimbledon
Surrey

Dear Father
Arrived Liverpool safe at 6.20 this morning. Feel very dirty. Would like a wash. Also,
breakfast which I'm just after. Fine day so far. More news soon.
Love to all
Frank

Henry Spooner, who received the postcard, was a retired inspector with the Metropolitan Police. Henry and his wife Sarah had 11 children. At least two sons became policemen, including George who was part of the Thames Police. He was killed in 1913 when he fell from a police boat after a collision with a barge near Southwark Bridge.

Archibald, another of Henry's sons, left England for Canada in 1911 at the age of 21. Over the following years he would return to England several times. In December 1914 he joined the Canadian army, giving his father's address as that on the postcard. In October 1918, while 'on active service' he returned to England and married Emily Samuda. Emily would have known the Spooner family very well – her family lived at 135 South Park Road and perhaps romance blossomed during a visit home. After the war, in 1919, Emily sailed to Canada and lived there for a short while before returning to England where she died in 1922.

A few months after arriving in Canada in 1907, Frank (who sent the postcard to his father) married Kathleen Murphy on Christmas Day. Kathleen was born in Lancashire, England and her father had been an officer in the Irish Constabulary. The couple eventually settled in Northumberland, Ontario where Frank became a postal clerk.

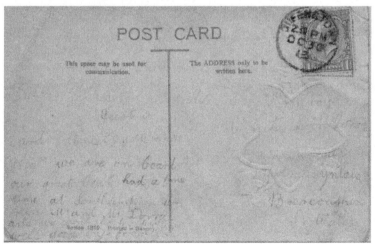

S015

30 October 1913
Mr S Pomroy
White Lion Cottage
Ynis-uchaf
Ystradgynlais
Breconshire
South Wales
England

Dear Stan
Just a card to let you know that we are on board our great boat. Had a fine time at
Southampton. We seen Mr and Mrs Dorroll and we went to the pictures.
Well goodbye from us.

Adolphus Pomroy sailed on RMS *Oceanic* and arrived in New York in November 1913. According to the ship's passenger lists he was a miner, and had brown hair and blue eyes. The record included that he had a friend in America, Stanley Rooke. Stanley's family lived in Tavistock, Devon and over the years after 1913 a number of Stanley's siblings also settled in America. Stanley would become a foreman in an auto factory in Detroit.

Adolphus (known as Harry) was born in Calstock, Cornwall (near Tavistock). By 1930 he had become a naturalised American citizen working in a copper mine in Montana where he lived with his wife, Alma Linkikoist, who was born in Sweden.

The card was sent to Harry's brother, Edwin, known as Stan. He had become a miner and lived in Wales where he eventually married Amy Little, a widow from Ilchester in Somerset.

Harry and Stan's father, Harry senior, was a gardener – as was his father, Henry. Harry senior's brother, Adolphus, emigrated to Australia in 1878 where he worked as a horticulturist growing fruit. He was regarded as a pioneer in his specialism, eventually working land in Lyrup, a town in south Australia. The family became so important to the region that there are roads named after them.

S020

10 April 1911
Mrs Munro
Waterhall Cottage
Chalfont St Peter
Buckinghamshire
England

Dear Mumsie
Just a line to let you know we going on alright. Have not quite settled yet, but hope to in a
day or two. We are getting fine weather now.
From us both
Lots of love

A David Munro appears in passenger lists for RMS *Hesperian*, arriving in Canada on 10 April 1911. Travelling with him is Thomas Munro. However, both men have Scotland as their place of birth and David, the son of Annie Munro, who received the card, was born in Thornton Heath, England in 1874.

After arriving in Canada, Annie's son travelled to America and worked in Massachusetts as an electrician. By 1920 he had become a naturalised citizen and lived with his wife, Nora (who had arrived in 1916). Also with the couple in 1920 was Annie, to whom the card was sent. She had also arrived in 1916 and appears in passenger lists aboard SS *St Louis* with David's sister, Christina. At this time Annie's status is given as housewife but by 1920 she was a widow. Her husband, David senior, last appears in the UK records in 1911.

Signing the postcard 'from us both' suggests David wasn't travelling alone. David had four sisters, but apart from Christina, they all remained in the UK.

According to the records I accessed, Annie never became a naturalised citizen but remained in America until her death in 1942. Christina worked as a maid and appears in passenger lists returning to England in 1923.

S011

SS Balmoral

1908
Mrs A Edwards
34 Maple St
Sheerness
Kent

Dear Ma
I am writing this to you half way between Shanklin & Ventnor at a little village called
Bonchurch built by St Boniface [in] *1070. This is the steamer we came over in.*
With love
Isabel

Isabel Edwards' mother, Mary Ann, was a widow, running a boarding house in Sheerness. She married barrister's clerk Edward Edwards in 1872. Her own father, Charles Carle, had been a musician in the army and is recorded as being a Chelsea Pensioner. Although Mary Ann was born in Sheerness, some of her siblings were born abroad – including two brothers who were born in Ceylon (Sri Lanka) in the 1840s.

Isabel married George Green in 1912. George had an engineering background and in 1911 he is listed as being an engineer with the Royal Fleet Auxiliary, boarding with the Edwards family at the address on the postcard.

His brother, Reginald, served in the RAF and in 1919 appears in an 'absent voter' register as a lieutenant. After the First World War he worked as an aircraft inspector in Surrey. Another brother, Harold, worked as an inspector of work in Portsmouth Dockyard.

The Isle of Wight is a popular holiday destination and even today, visitors will use a ferry service from locations along the Dorset/Hampshire coast. On a clear day it's possible to see the Isle of Wight from Swanage, where I grew up. As a child my family had holidays on the island – catching the ferry from Lymington in Hampshire. That 50 or so miles, plus the ferry crossing, was enough of a journey to make us feel we were definitely on holiday – even though we could see Swanage when we were on the right side of the island!

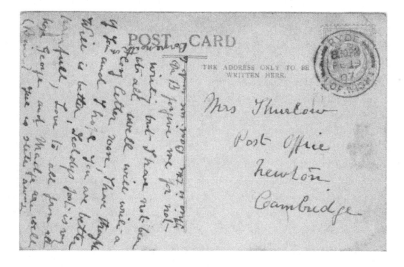

S023

SS Balmoral

19 February 1907
Mrs Thurlow
Post Office
Newton
Cambridge

Dear B
Forgive me for not writing but I have not been at all well. Will write a long letter now I
have thought of you, and I hope you are better. Will is better, Teddy's foot is very painful.
Love to all from all. Hope George and Madge are well (Bina). … is still away.
This is the boat we went to Bournemouth on.

Mrs Thurlow – Elizabeth née Trudgill – was the postmistress in Newton where she lived with her husband, Alfred, and their daughter, Madeline. Alfred was a carpenter by trade who also farmed. His father, Thomas, was a butler but before that, in 1851, he was a servant, working in St John's College Cambridge. Thirty years later, he appears as a butler working for Christopher Pemberton, in Newton Hall, Cambridge. Pemberton's daughter, Henrietta, married first class cricketer Spencer Montagu, son of Baron Rokeby – an MP who is described as being a 'faithful follower of Pitt'. He represented constituencies in Cornwall and was a friend and supporter of William Wilberforce – a leader in the fight to abolish slavery.

Elizabeth Trudgill's sister, Sabina (Bina) married greengrocer William Sheppard in 1903 and the couple lived in Ryde, Isle of Wight, where William was born in 1856. Before their marriage, Sabina had worked as a servant in Bournemouth. After her husband's death in 1927, Sabina returned to the Cambridgeshire area and lived with her niece, Madeline.

S005A

SS Lucania

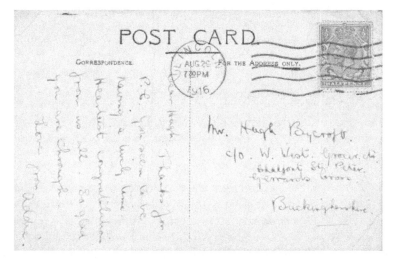

S005B

RMS Franconia

1 July 1905
Master Bycroft
C/o H Bycroft, Esq
High Street
Lincoln

Dear Hughie
This is the big boat that takes us to New York. Will you tell Father that we received his
letter & PC & thank him very much. The boat sails 4.30 pm.
Love to you all.
Addie

29 August 1916
Mr Hugh Bycroft
C/o W West Grocer etc
Chalfont St Peter
Gerrards Cross
Buckinghamshire

Dear Hugh
Thanks for PC. You seem to be having a lively time. Heartiest congratulations from us
all. So glad you are through.
Love from Addie

As many of the postcards I research are often sent by relatives of the recipient, I was surprised not to find Addie in Hugh's family tree. However, the passenger lists for SS *Lucania* provided me with the information to trace Addie and her family.

Addie was born in Australia in 1884. After the death of her father her mother's brother, William McPherson, accepted responsibility for her and her siblings' education. Addie was the middle child of William Eady and Barbara née McPherson. Barbara's brother, William, was a successful engineer in Australia and arranged for Addie's brother, Marshall, to live in England to learn about the work of foundries.

In 1903 he was sent to Ruston & Hornsby in Lincoln. He returned to Australia four years later with the experience and skills needed to help with his uncle's business.

During Marshall's time in England his mother and sisters sailed to a number of locations around the world; later, Marshall would also travel extensively. His time in Lincoln wasn't perhaps a lonely one – clearly his family stayed there for some time and seemed to have forged a good relationship with Hugh and his family.

As well as being a successful businessman, Sir William McPherson became a politician and in 1928 was elected Premier of Victoria. His term in office was a short one of less than two years. He was known as a philanthropist and donated a substantial amount to found the Emily McPherson School of Domestic Economy, named after his wife whom he'd married in 1892 at St Andrew's Cathedral, Sydney. He also funded the Jessie McPherson wing of the now-demolished Queen Victoria Hospital, named after his mother.

Hugh Bycroft, who received the postcards, was born in 1900. As an adult, he eventually ran a sportswear and toy shop on the High Street in Lincoln. But this wasn't his first job. He had trained as a pharmacist but was sacked, according to his grandson, for putting a laxative in his boss' tea. Opening the shop in Lincoln was an astute move. He added sportswear and equipment to the stock during the Second World War and this attracted business from those serving at the nearby airbases.

In 1901, *Lucania* was the first Cunard liner to be fitted with a Marconi wireless system. The second was RMS *Campania* and the ships made history by exchanging the first wireless transmitted ice bulletin. Not long afterwards, *Lucania* became the first ship to publish an onboard newsletter, created from wireless messages received at sea.

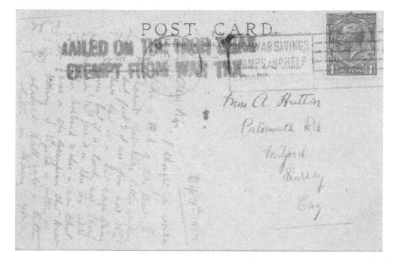

S021

RMS Minnedosa

9 September 1919
Miss A Hutton
Portsmouth Road
Milford
Surrey
England

Dear Nan
I thought you would like a PC of the boat.
I haven't felt like letter writing but Jack and I are fine now.
We have had it a bit rough coming over but it is lovely now.
Mary from Mrs J's is on here too with her husband and also a man that was on the
Grampian that knew Henry. I hope he is getting on alright.
Will write a letter later on.
Hoping you are well.
Love from both, Lily

Lily was sailing to Canada with her husband, Irish-born Jack (John) Kernohan. When the couple married earlier that year, Jack worked as a shipping clerk. He'd already lived in Canada before the couple sailed in 1919 and had enlisted in the Canadian army in 1914.

The card was received by Lily's sister, Annie, who was a domestic servant. Lily wasn't the only member of her family to emigrate – brothers Percy and William would emigrate to Australia. Percy, a baker, appears in the passenger lists for SS *Wakool*, sailing in 1911. In 1927 he returned to England for a visit and sailed back to Australia with his wife, Hilda, and their two children.

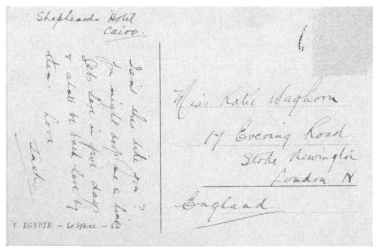

S104

The Sphinx, Egypt

Miss Katie Waghorn
17 Evering Road
Stoke Newington
London N
England

Shepheard's Hotel, Cairo
Isn't this like you? You might drop me a line. Seb here in five days and I shall be back
here by then.
Love Jack

Katie Waghorn was born in 1897 and her father, Henry, was an embroiderer. Records show that he made gold braid, possibly for military uniforms. In more recent times, this intricate work came under the spotlight during the coronation of King Charles III. The embellishments on the uniforms worn during the procession were made by a family-run firm in Tottenham.

Henry Waghorn's first wife died when he was 47. A year later, he married Henrietta Kaye, Katie's mother. Henry had at least six children with his first wife, Ellen Courtney. In 1901, Helen was a theatre attendant in London and lived with her two sisters, Florence and Edith, who were office workers.

There's no record of Katie marrying anyone by the name of Jack and it's impossible to know exactly when he sent her the card. However, her mother appears in electoral records at the address in 1915. Earlier records show the family in Aldwych when Henry and Henrietta both worked as embroiderers.

It might be that Jack was in Egypt during the First World War. Shepheard's Hotel was a grand building in Cairo and during the war it was used to accommodate British officers. It's acknowledged in the novel and film, *The English Patient*, set just before the outbreak of the Second World War. However, the hotel from where Jack sent his postcard was destroyed in the 1950s during riots that affected some 750 businesses, so a hotel in Paris was used for the location scenes. Still, the film does recreate the atmosphere just before the outbreak of the Second World War.

Katie took good care of Jack's postcard. Although the stamp has been removed, the card itself is almost unmarked.

S101

Corcovado, Rio de Janeiro

29 November 1911
Mrs Holmes
Connaught House
Attleborough
Norfolk
England

Have been on top.

Seeing the handwriting on the 1911 census matched that on the postcard, should have made it clear who sent the card from Brazil. However, the return was completed on behalf of Thomas Holmes, the head of the household, and he merely signed it. Thomas and his wife Mary had two of their ten children living with them in 1911 – including son Frederick, a marine engineer, and the sender of the card. By 1939, he had married, retired and lived with his also retired variety entertainer wife, Hollie, in Worthing.

Although Frederick's family lived in Norfolk, they eventually moved to Bath. Earlier, they had lived in Cambridge where all the children were born. Thomas was a grocer by trade and his shop in Sidney Street employed several men and boys. The family lived above the shop.

There wasn't anything special about the Holmes family, but I wondered if I might be that 'one click away' from discovering something remarkable, and that's what happened when I looked into the family business.

The Holmes' business appears in several online articles – mainly on local history websites. There's a mention of Mary and Minnie, the eldest daughters, in an article about Indian cricketer Ranjitsinhji Jadeja. Ranji, as he was known, studied at Cambridge and became, it's believed, besotted with Mary, giving her expensive gifts of jewellery. He even paid for a train (not just a carriage) to take her to London for a trip. While studying at Cambridge University, Ranji developed his skills as a cricketer and would eventually play for Sussex and England – playing against Australia in 15 Test matches. He was regarded as the best Indian player of his time. His relationship with Mary wasn't widely known but is confirmed by letters he sent to her, which her family eventually gave to Trinity College, Cambridge. Mary would ultimately marry William Clarke and it's believed Ranji continued his friendship with Minnie and other women in England. Eventually he returned to India where, by a quirk of fate, he became Maharaja of Nawangar through a distant ancestral connection.

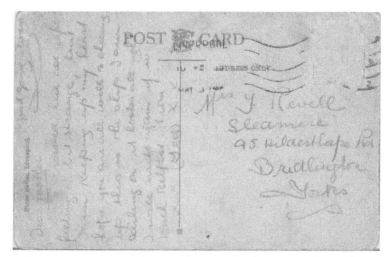

S026

S.S. Lake Manitoba

Mrs F Revell
Sleamere
95 Hilderthorpe Road
Bridlington
Yorks

Just going aboard.

Dear Mother
Arrived here all safe. Feeling a bit strange, but I am keeping up my heart. Hope you are
all well & cheering up. This is the ship I am sailing on. It looks all right. I will write
again if we touch Belfast.
From XX Ted XX

Ted (Edwin) was writing to his mother in May 1914 when he sailed from Liverpool to Canada. He was leaving behind his wife, Lilian, and their two young daughters, Gladys and Vera.

In the UK, he worked as a railway porter and continued working on railways in Canada. A year after Ted left England, Lilian and the girls sailed to Canada aboard SS *Missanabie* and the family settled in Belleville, Ontario. Ted was one of 13 children and by 1911, his parents (Frank and Frances) recorded that seven had died.

A son, Frank junior, also sailed to Canada. In 1929 he declared that the purpose of his trip was 'to settle' in Canada. However, he eventually returned to Hull. Another brother, Harold, had left England a year before Ted. When he enlisted in the Canadian army in 1916, his records showed that he had a number of tattoos, including one of a pair of hands and a flag – not dissimilar, perhaps, to the 'hands across the sea' image used on so many postcards, including the one his brother sent home.

SS *Lake Manitoba* was part of the Canadian Pacific Line and a few months after Ted's voyage, the ship was requisitioned by the Admiralty.

S028

PS Princess Joséphine

1906
Mrs Curtis
108 Carisbrook Road
Liverpool N
England

Just leaving for Vienna. Much love to all.
Wilson

Wilson Curtis sent the postcard to his mother, Caroline née Wilson. Wilson was born in Dartmouth, Devon in 1866 and would become a captain in the Merchant Navy. His brother, Foster, would also become a mariner. In 1902, a presentation of a gold medal and a diploma was made to Foster in recognition of his services in rescuing 19 of the crew from a German four-masted ship, *Euterpe*, off the coast of the Isles of Scilly. The ship was carrying coal from Wales to Chile when an explosion caused devastating damage with the loss of six lives.

William and Foster's father, John Curtis, was born in Devon in 1831 and he was a master mariner. He died in 1885 in Gibraltar Bay from injuries sustained when he was washed overboard from Cunard's SS *Sidon*. Newspapers reported that he was supervising the dropping of the anchor and lost his footing. Although no one witnessed the accident, he was soon missed and on spotting John in the water, the ship's cook jumped overboard with a buoy. According to reports, there was a 'heroic attempt' to rescue John, who was still conscious. The cook, John Watkinson, managed to haul John on to some rocks where they were rescued the following day by SS *India*. Sadly, John had succumbed to his injuries, thought to have been received when his head hit the anchor's chain.

A few months later, *Sidon* suffered another tragedy. Forty-one crew and 14 passengers were sailing off the coast of Spain when the ship hit a ledge of rocks and was wrecked, resulting in the loss of some passengers and crew.

Caroline, John's widow, appears in the official records as either the head of the household (in John's absence) or as a widow. She grew up knowing how perilous her family's situation could be – her own father, Robert Wilson, was a master mariner.

By the time the card was sent in 1906, Wilson had been married for ten years to Australian Charlotte Bindon, whom he married in New South Wales.

S030

RMS Empress of Britain

27 October 1911
Miss Lucy Will
3 Sams Lane
West Bromwich
Staffordshire

Dear Lucy
Just a line to say I arrived safe at Quebec Sat. I am sorry but I had more to pack up than
I thought, so that is why I didn't keep my promise the other Wednesday. I am feeling alright
now, hoping you are.
I remain yours truly
Fred X

Sams Lane is an area that's been completely transformed – cramped housing was replaced with industrial units and rows of modern houses in the 1960s. In 1911, 3 Sams Lane was home to several families living in numbers 3 to 3D. Unfortunately, none had a Lucy within their households. Further along the lane, I found Lucy Wilkes at number 96. She lived there with her parents, George and Victoria. George was a labourer and Victoria née Barratt was a midwife. By 1911 they'd had 12 children and six, a tragic number, had died. Lucy, who was the youngest and still living at home, was employed in carpentry work. Two of her brothers, James and William, worked for a printer.

Of course, none of this confirmed that Lucy Wilkes was the Lucy mentioned in the card. However, in 1915, Lucy Wilkes married Frederick Caddick. Could he be the Fred who sent the postcard? In 1911 he lived with his parents, John and Esther, in Temple Street – just a mile or so from Sams Lane. At this time, John was a cooper and Fred was a fitter.

On 26 October 1911, Fred Caddick arrived in Canada aboard RMS *Empress of Britain*. On 21 December 1914 he returned to England, via New York, aboard SS *Orduña*.

After their marriage in 1915, Lucy and Fred lived in the same area they had known as children and where Fred worked as a spring tool maker.

I'll never know why the card was addressed to number 3 – perhaps Lucy's family moved between when the census was taken and Fred sent the postcard (which has happened in other families I've researched). Perhaps Fred simply made a mistake.

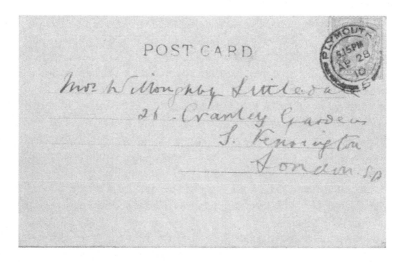

S031

SS Arabia

27 April 1910
Mrs Willoughby Littledale
26 Cranley Gardens
S Kensington
London

We expect to reach Plymouth tomorrow and Tilbury on Friday about 2 p.m.

Although I couldn't find the Littledale family at the address in the 1911 census return, a directory listed Willoughby Aston Littledale there in 1910. Willoughby was the passenger on SS *Arabia* with his son, also named Willoughby.

Willoughby Aston married Violet Thursby, daughter of John Hardy Thursby, the 1st Baronet of Ormerod House and Holmhurst. The Thursby family had made their fortune from coal and in 1888 John gifted a large parcel of land for the creation of Queen's Park, in Burnley. In today's money, this amounted to a value of more than £3 million.

The Thursby family appears in several online records in America where research links them as descendants of Edward IV and Henry VIII. It's surprising how many American trees I've looked at include this claim – of course, I cannot verify any of that content.

Willoughby's family was no less notable than his wife's. He was born in Lancashire in 1857 and, like his father Henry, became a barrister and the family's lineage is recorded in *Burke's*. Willoughby wasn't the only member of his family to live in a grand house – several siblings lived in the richest parts of London.

Willoughby junior, who had sailed with his father to England from India via Aden, Port Said, Gibraltar and Marseilles, served in the First World War and was killed in France in 1918. Willoughby senior and Violet had a daughter, Eleanor, and in 1920 she married a doctor – Humphrey Pollock. While still a medical student, Humphrey served in the First World War as a captain with the Royal Army Medical Corps in France.

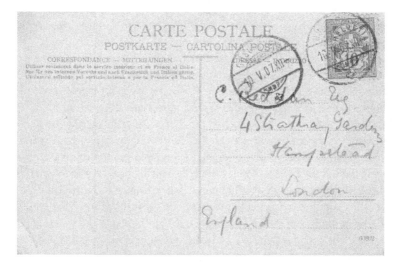

S100

Lucerne, Switzerland

10 May 1907
C Reddan Esq
4 Strathray Gardens
Hampstead
London
England

This gives a good idea of this railway.
Yours
Dick

Charles Reddan died just weeks before the 1911 census might have confirmed him at Strathray Gardens. His father, William, was there in 1911 with his wife, Emma, and their three surviving children – all daughters. Charles' two brothers had also died by 1911 – one in infancy, the other as an adult.

William is recorded as being a draper – which wasn't an uncommon business at the time. Drapers provided an essential service in the Victorian and Edwardian eras. However, William Reddan's business, The Emporium, was more than just a typical shop. He employed a team of assistants and it was the customers who raised the profile of the Reddan family's work.

William's business address was in Soho and his clientele included Princess Mary and a young Winston Churchill. The large site, in Old Compton Street, was sold after William's death and cleared for the building of the Prince Edward Theatre. William's brother, Charles, had his own business in London and he died within a few days of his nephew in 1911. Charles junior, who received the postcard, is recorded as dying at Strathray Gardens and his uncle, just a few roads away, in Queen's Crescent. According to his death certificate, Charles junior had suffered for 18 years from a condition that affected his kidneys and this had worsened in the week before his death.

S054

17 March 1909
Mrs Saxton
349 Hendricks Street
Detroit
Michigan
USA

46 Shakespeare Street
Beckett Street
Leeds
Yorkshire

Dear Sister
Please … long letter. I have got inflammation in the eyes and I can't bear to write much.
Was sorry to hear about R. It appears you will always have to work. But hope for the best.
Shall be pleased to hear from you soon.
Your loving sister

Martha Greaves, née Dyson, sender of the postcard and sister to Elizabeth, lived in Shakespeare Street with her husband, Thomas, and their four children.

The Dyson sisters were born in Leeds and their father was a labourer. In 1873, Elizabeth married Henry Saxton and the couple had several children. Her son Robert was born in 1879 and he appears in the 1910 US census living in Detroit. A year later he married German-born divorcée Augusta Heneke. Augusta's daughter, Leona, would eventually take her stepfather's surname. Robert died in 1921 when his son with Augusta, Ralph, would have been a toddler.

The name Elizabeth Saxton appears in passenger lists as sailing across the Atlantic to visit Michigan. One states she is visiting her brother J Saxton. This could be her brother-in-law, Joseph. However, there's no record of him leaving Yorkshire, where he died in the 1920s. Just to complicate the story further, he married Frances Greaves, Martha's sister-in-law.

The only records that show the family at the address in America are directories. In 1908 Robert lived there alone and a year later, Elizabeth is at the address, but on *her* own. Was this what Martha was referring to – that Robert had moved out and Elizabeth was responsible for the home? In 1910 he is working in a stove factory and living as a boarder at Augusta's house. He marries her the following year. Whatever the circumstances, by 1911 Elizabeth had returned to England and was living with the Greaves family including her sister in Shakespeare Street. She was still working as a dressmaker – a job recorded in the passenger lists and earlier records.

AMERICAN LINE U.S. MAIL TWIN-SCREW STEAMER "PHILADELPHIA"

Going home for a six weeks vacation.
The idea is immense after 3 years absence.
Thanks for your suggestion as to getting fresh
air.   Mid-Atlantic Apr. 4-07   F.H.B.

POST CARD.

THE ADDRESS ONLY TO BE WRITTEN ON THIS SIDE.

Miss Cordelia Bertch

Solon Springs,

Wis. U.S.A.

S045

SS Philadelphia

Miss Cordelia Bertch
Solon Springs
Wisconsin
USA

Mid-Atlantic
4 Apr 1907
Going home for a six weeks vacation. The idea is immense after 3 years absence.
Thanks for your suggestion as to getting fresh air.
FHB...

With only the initials and abbreviated surname, I was still able to find Fernley Hope Banbury in the passenger lists for SS *Philadelphia*, and with the knowledge that he hadn't returned home for three years, I soon confirmed I had the correct passenger.

Fernley was born in Cornwall in 1881 and his father and brothers were farmers. Despite not having returned home for several years, over the years that followed he sailed across the Atlantic multiple times, including in early 1910 aboard RMS *Laurentic* – returning to America with his wife of only a few weeks.

Christine Bickle was born in Cornwall but grew up in Devon. Her father, Jebus Bickle, was part of an engineering family whose company built engines that worked the mines in Cornwall, the docks in Plymouth and elsewhere, including overseas. It's through Jebus' company that Fernley and Christine met. Although the couple lived in America, they often returned to Cornwall. After visiting England in 1914, they returned to America aboard RMS *Lusitania*.

So many of the stories I research involve family members affected by chance. As a young man, Fernley had intended to sail from Southampton to India to work in a gold mine as an engineer but, through an extended trip to say goodbye to friends and family, he missed the boat. Another opportunity came his way in 1904, and he left Cornwall for America, where a period of intense study led to a degree in engineering. Fernley stayed in America, developing an industrial mixer. By 1916, the Banbury Mixer had begun its life, as part of the manufacture of rubber products, primarily tyres.

A biography about Fernley, published in 1962, has a foreword written by EJ Thomas, then chairman of The Goodyear Tire and Rubber Company – such was the importance to the tyre industry of Fernley's mixer. The chairman wrote, 'The word Banbury is one of the first to be learned in the vocabulary of the modern rubber industry'.

The rapid development of the motor industry took full advantage of Fernley's mixer and, later, more modern versions still bear his name.

Banbury: The Master Mixer was written by DH Killeffer who retired to the same part of Florida as Fernley and Christine, and became a good friend. His book has family photographs, including one of Fernley and Christine celebrating their golden wedding anniversary on a cruise.

Christine's brother, Jebus Trinery Bickle, also emigrated from England to America and worked as an engineer in a copper mine in Texas. He married his wife, Florence Hutton, in Mexico where their first child was born.

Unfortunately I was unable to confirm with whom Fernley was sharing the news of his visit home.

Gletscherbesteigung - Ascension d'un Glacier

S108

Glacier

This is to make you feel nice and cool.
We arrived here all safely and are enjoying ourselves immensely.
We have to skip up mountains like two-year-olds.
We went halfway up and slid about on a glacier.
I sat down on it and had to be pulled off by guides!

Posted to Coventry in 1906

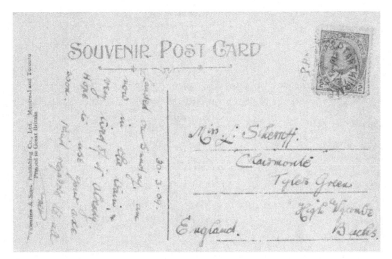

S035

Elevators, Fort William, on Canadian Pacific Railway

30 March 1909
Miss L Sherriff
Clairmonte
Tylers Green
High Wycombe
Buckinghamshire
England

Landed on Sunday, am now in the train, & very tired of it already.
Hope to use your axe soon.
Kind regards to all.

With such lovely handwriting – and the image of an axe-wielding visitor to Canada – I had high hopes for this story and revealing who had packed an axe in their trunk. Alas it was not to be.

In 1911, second-generation confectioner Joseph Sherriff lived with his wife, Clara, and several of their eight children at the address on the card. It wasn't difficult to find all the children – some had left home but their common work as confectioners made confirming them the easiest part of this puzzle.

Joseph junior was with his own family, as was Arthur (whose father-in-law was also a confectioner). Student Ernest was still living at home, and he would later become a merchant in India. Of the sisters, none seemed to be a match for the recipient of the card – but Adeline, Edith, Margaret, Selina and Frances could all have had 'pet' names.

Who might have sent the card? Knowing they had arrived in Canada on a certain date didn't help – nor did searching the Canadian census records for the following year (the information includes the year of arrival). Checking the handwriting of the spouses of the sisters that had married was also a dead end. Whoever sent the card must have been embarking on an adventure – something requiring a new axe – and the card had been kept in excellent condition, so the recipient must have had a strong relationship with the sender.

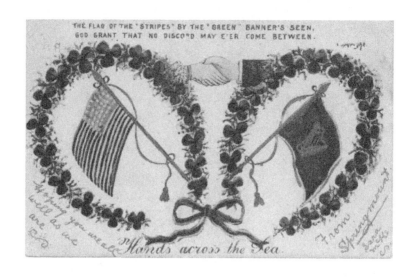

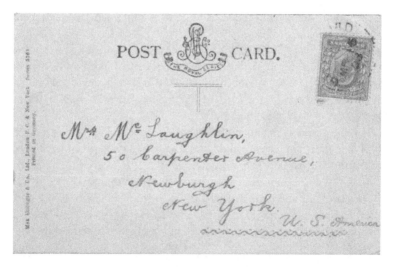

S049

Mrs McLaughlin
50 Carpenter Avenue
Newburgh
New York
US America

Hoping you are all well as we are.
From
Springmount
Sara McK...

By rights, this card shouldn't be included because the information I've discovered is sparse at best. Jane McLaughlin was born in Ireland and arrived in America in around 1879 with her husband, James. Directories for the Newburgh area, show that James McLaughlin was a labourer. The couple lived at the address on the card for a number of years and Jane remained there after James' death in 1888. Jane was still in Carpenter Avenue for the 1920 census and with her is daughter Mary. Later, Jane would live with Mary and her son-in-law, Edgar Lynn, who was a salesman.

Although I tried to trace the family back to Springmount, it was impossible to make a positive connection. It must have been lovely for Jane to receive the card – knowing the trouble Sara had taken to make it extra special.

S055

16 December 1908
Miss Pullen
429 Auburn Avenue
Buffalo
America
NY

Dear Emily
Just to wish you all the happiness of the season.
With love from Auntie & Uncle A & C Haywood

Emily's parents, Alfred and Emily, sailed for Canada aboard SS *Sardinian* in November 1886. With them was baby Edith who died a few months after the family arrived. In Canada, the couple had at least four more children, including Emily in 1889. For reasons that aren't known, the family moved to America in 1898 where Alfred worked in construction. In 1911, two of their children, Rosana and Alfred, died. They were both in their early twenties. A newspaper obituary published in August for Rosana mentions that she was a 'highly esteemed member of the popular set'. She passed away from typhoid at the address on the postcard. In that month alone there were 15 local deaths from the disease. Although Alfred's cause of death isn't known, he died earlier in the year when the disease was on the increase in the area.

It wasn't unusual to discover that members of a working class family returned to England for visits from their new homes abroad. In 1910, Emily's father appears in the passenger lists for RMS *Lusitania*, sailing back to New York from Liverpool. He is described as being 5'7" tall, with brown hair, grey eyes and a medium complexion. He was in possession of $50.

Also aboard the ship was Robert Pound. He was born in 1891 in the Worcestershire area – not far from where the Pullen family had lived. Robert is described as having blue eyes, a fair complexion and fair hair. He was required to provide the name of a resident in America – Alfred Pullen. Robert appears in the 1910 census living with the Pullen family in Auburn Avenue. The following year, Robert married Emily – the recipient of the postcard.

Emily's mother, Emily, was born in Herefordshire in 1864. Her father, Alfred Haywood, is listed as a tailor and then a grocer. In 1911 he appears in the census return as a widower living with his farmer son Charles and Charles' wife Annie – who sent her niece the postcard.

S067

Ramsden Dock, Barrow

25 September 1906
Master James A Wells
Chapel Place
Norwood Green
Halifax

Have just landed here. I very much regret you are not with us. I expected you. I do hope
you are better. Have just seen the vessel Natal we saw launched last year. It is not yet
finished.
Kind regards
Your Uncle

James Wells was only 14 when his Uncle James sent the postcard. James junior lived with his uncle, brother and widowed father, Levi. Also at the address in 1911 was Martha, James and Levi's unmarried sister. Martha and Levi were pattern dyers, and Levi's eldest son, George, would become a foreman in the same industry.

James, who received the card, studied as a bookkeeper, but by 1939 he was a retired musician. The family lived in the Brighouse area of Halifax, perhaps best known for the Brighouse and Rastrick Brass Band. Although it would have been lovely to confirm a connection, James' musical output isn't known.

There are some interesting details added to the postcard, perhaps by uncle and nephew. In particular, those of the ship possibly depicted in the postcard's image. HMS *Natal* was launched on 30 September 1905 and was sunk ten years later in water off the Cromarty Firth by an 'internal explosion'. More than 390 civilians and crew lost their lives – including women and children who were visiting the ship. The site of the wreck is now protected.

PS *Duchess of Buccleuch* was owned by the Barrow Steam Navigation Company. She was bought in 1903 as PS *Rouen* and taken out of service in 1909.

S091

RMS Baltic

6 March 1910
Miss M Hughes
88 Hazlewell Road
Putney
London
SW

Dear Mag
Just a card to thank you for the tie and card. I am sending you this to see what Becc went on. Poor Becc, she broke down just before we came off the ship but she seemed allright when she started out! She got the PO and is going to write to you from Queenstown. Mother will send you a long letter later on. From your loving brother Charlie.
PS
I went to the panto on Friday. It was grand and saw Ciss on Saturday. She looks as well as ever.

One of the most endearing aspects of the postcards I research is discovering how people were addressed by their friends and families. Official records confirm their names, but is that how they were known?

Mag Hughes wasn't at the address on the card in any official records. The 1911 census shows that the head of the household was a solicitor and he employed a number of servants. Of course, Mag might well have worked for the family between the 1901 and 1911 census returns.

Was Becc Mag and Charlie's sister and did she sail on the ship?

Assuming Becc might be Rebecca, I searched the passenger lists and once I'd discounted some through their ages, I was left with six or so possible matches. Rebecca Griffiths was 35 years of age, from Wales and was married. She declared that a Mrs C Hughes was known to her in the UK. There was also an address for Mrs Hughes – but it was illegible.

Creating a tree for Rebecca led me to discover her husband was George Griffiths and that only three months after she returned to him in America, she gave birth to a son, Emil. With such an unusual name, I was able to trace him in passenger lists, sailing on RMS *Carmania* in 1913 with Rebecca. This time, her mother's address was clearly written and I traced the family to Overton in Wales. Charlie, who sent the postcard, was a blacksmith (as was his father) and he married Mary Rogers in 1920. The handwriting on the card is a perfect match for his signature in the marriage register.

Although Mag (as Margaret) appears with the family in 1891 when she was four, there was little to find for her in the official records. In 1901 she was a servant working as a laundress for a laundryman and market gardener in Liverpool. We know that she later moved to the address on the card, but after that it wasn't possible to find accurate sightings.

ROYAL MAIL MOTOR VESSEL "ASTURIAS" (TWIN SCREW 22,071 TONS) SOUTH AMERICAN SERVICE

S075

RMMV Asturias

22 July 1929
Miss ME King
Rushmere Hall
Near Ipswich
Suffolk
England

Asturias

Thanks so much for your letter. You surely have had some letters from me! We're just off on holiday – for a week in Montevideo – a day's trip across the river. We're enjoying boat life once again. Wish we were coming to Southampton.
Love Ruth

Margaret King was born in 1902 into a family of farmers. Both her grandfathers farmed several hundred acres in Suffolk and employed more than 12 men each. She was the daughter of Benjamin King and Emily née Everett and it's the Everett branch of the family that proved the more fascinating to explore.

Margaret's grandfather was Robert Lacey Everett – a farmer and politician. In 1880 he stood, unsuccessfully, for Parliament as a farmers' candidate (some records show him as a Liberal). Five years later he was successful, although he lost his Woodbridge seat the following year during a general election. He was also successful in 1892, but ousted in 1906 – ten years before his death.

Robert had several children, including journalist Robert Everett. Robert junior lived in Fowey, Cornwall and was a great supporter of local projects – including the cottage hospital where he eventually died in the 1960s.

He received the Silver Acorn badge from the Boy Scouts' Association for outstanding service and was also the recipient of an award for his work with the British Legion, especially in the founding of a branch in Tywardreath.

Robert wasn't the only sibling to be associated with the Scouting movement. His brother, Percy, was an editor, working for publisher Lord Pearson who founded the *Daily Express*. Lord Pearson invited Percy to a dinner party where he met Robert Baden-Powell. Over the months that followed, an idea that became the Boy Scouts was formed. Percy was invited to help and attended the first camp on Brownsea Island in Poole Harbour – an invitation he thought he received because of his farming background.

As Deputy Chief Scout, Percy would later record those early years in a short book *The First Ten Years* and recalled how he worked on the movement's publications, encouraging Baden-Powell to meet their deadlines. He would later write: *He was more business-like than most authors … It was fascinating to watch him writing and sketching, now with the right hand, now with the left, for, as you all know, he was ambidextrous.*

Percy would eventually lead his own Group – 1st Elstree, which is where he lived with his wife. He was proud of the work he and others undertook, especially when the Scouts were employed during the First World War to help in their local communities. Those who had passed beyond their Scouting years, served as soldiers. Lieutenant JHS Dimmer of the King's Royal Rifle Corps was the first Scout to win the VC and his was the first Cross awarded for fighting in Flanders.

Percy was knighted in 1930 for his services to the Scouting movement.

I never discovered who Ruth might have been – the passenger lists available were very incomplete. Margaret never married and she died in Rushmere in the 1980s.

RMMV *Asturias* was launched from Belfast's shipyards. After being requisitioned by the Admiralty for service during the Second World War she was attached to the South Atlantic Station before being transferred to the West Africa Command. Ultimately, she finished her days in Faslane, Scotland where she was to be scrapped. That work had begun when the producers of *A Night to Remember* paid for the use of the ship's portside (the starboard was already being dismantled). *Asturias* was not the first choice for the role – ship owners were reluctant to have their name associated with the tragedy. But the producers moved fast, paid the fee and completed the paperwork before there could be any objections raised. The ship's side was repainted, courtesy of students from Glasgow's university.

S019

RMS Metagama

Arrived here last night tired and dirty. A stranger in a strange land.
The US Customs took my brandy from me.
My large trunks have not turned up yet.
Got wet through this morning.
Much love to both.
Have had a poisoned finger.

Posted to Cumberland.

U.S.M.S.S. "NEW YORK"
PASSING NETLEY HOSPITAL.

POST CARD.   CARTE POSTALE.

UNIVERSAL POSTAL UNION.

For Inland Postage In United States and
Great Britain this space may be used
for communications

The Address only to be written here.

We have several
children running
about on board = just
about your own age
Simply lovely weather
Best love from
Daddie

To Miss Abbott
Spenser Lodge
Spenser Road
Harpenden
Herts
England -

S059

USMSS New York

27 September 1908
To Miss Abbott
Spenser Lodge
Spenser Road
Harpenden
Herts
England

We have several children running about on board – just about your own age.
Simply lovely weather.
Best love from Daddie

As well as tracking people through official records, it's also very satisfying to see their handwriting and the 1911 census is particularly useful for this. Usually, but not always, the head of the household completed this return and it's often the first opportunity to see an ancestor's handwriting.

When I found the Abbott family at the address in 1911, I was disappointed to see that Mary Abbott had completed the return, although her husband, Frederick, was listed as the head of the household – and, in theory, present. The other family member was Sylvia, who was 13 – making her eight when 'Daddie' sent the card. Mary recorded her age as being 47 – six years older than Frederick. Another record that's accessible to family historians where you will find an ancestor's handwriting – or at least their signature – is the marriage register. By 1911, Frederick and Mary had been married for 13 years and I traced their marriage in 1898. At this time Mary is recorded as being only one year older than the groom. And, most disappointingly, Frederick's signature didn't match the handwriting on the postcard. Did I have the correct marriage record? The bride was Mary Grimsdale and from Sylvia's birth certificate I was able to confirm that I did have the correct marriage.

Researching Mary's life, I discovered that other records had varying ages. In only the very early census returns were the ages declared correctly. Her birth was registered in 1862 – eight years before Frederick's. I found Frederick Abbott aboard USMSS *New York* in 1908. He was sailing without his family and was possibly going to America on business. He appears in other passenger lists at other times, but the one for 1908 records him as being 5'5" tall, having brown eyes, a dark complexion and dark hair. Frederick was a manufacturer of oilskins and waterproof materials. With others, he ran the company Abbott, Anderson & Abbott, which began trading in the 1860s in Hertfordshire. I'll never know why the handwriting on the postcard doesn't match Frederick's in official records. In the passenger lists, his wife is recorded as being his nearest relative in the UK, at the address to which the card was sent.

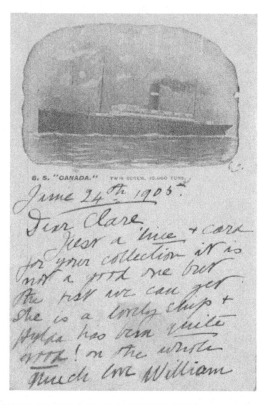

S050

SS Canada

24 June 1905
Miss C Willes
Newbold Comyn
Leamington
England

Dear Clare
Just a line & card for your collection. It is not a good one but the best we can get. She is a
lovely ship and Hylda has been quite good! on the whole.
Much love
William

William and Clare Willes were siblings – born in 1879 and 1884 – and Newbold Comyn was their family's ancestral home for almost 400 years. Their grandfather, Edward, was a landowner and great benefactor to the area. He gifted almost 11 acres of land for the Newbold Gardens, later renamed the Jephson Gardens – in honour of Dr Henry Jephson, recognised as the chief promoter of the town's spa water and 'benefactor to the poor'. Edward Willes is remembered in the gardens through an obelisk, erected in his memory in 1875.

Newbold Comyn was a substantial property but it was eventually sold to the local authority and demolished in the 1960s to make way for a housing estate.

William and Clare's mother, Alice Cope, was no stranger to great houses. In 1699 her ancestor Sir John Cope bought Bramshill House in Hampshire. The Cope family lived there until the 1930s when the property and estate was sold. The house was used as a Red Cross maternity hospital during the Second World War and was, for a while, the home of exiled King Michael of Romania.

William was sailing to Canada with his wife, Hilda/Hylda. He worked overseas as an engineer and the couple's children were born in Canada and America. William died in Newbold Comyn in the 1950s.

Clare had another brother, Richard. After being invalided out from the Royal Navy, Richard became a barrister. With his wife Marian, he had one son, Peter, who was educated at Stowe in Buckinghamshire where he met the actor David Niven. The pair would become friends and Niven's later success influenced Peter's choice of career.

Before the Second World War, Peter appeared in a number of films – including *The Dawn Patrol* with David Niven, Erroll Flynn and Basil Rathbone. Peter would also make films with Olivia de Havilland and Clark Gable. He appeared in two of Basil Rathbone's Sherlock Holmes films.

In 1937 he was returning to England aboard SS *Paris*. Travelling with him was close friend Frank Vosper. Frank was also an actor – and writer –

appearing on stage and screen, even performing in his own plays and their celluloid versions. He was known to be a practical joker and on one of the final days of the passage, he climbed through a window in the lounge where he and Peter had been socialising with other passengers. There was no deck on the other side and he fell overboard to his death. The subsequent inquest investigated the idea that the action was deliberate and that he had committed suicide. Witnesses discounted this and said it was typical of his character to lark around. Whatever his real intention, his body was found off Beachy Head, Sussex a few weeks later and the incident was eventually deemed to be an accident. Of course, today it's not possible to open such windows – safety is paramount.

Peter remained in the entertainment industry, becoming head of Yorkshire TV. During his tenure he was executive producer for many memorable programmes including *Hadleigh* and *Raffles* (starring Gerald Harper and Anthony Valentine).

Although I don't always research all the siblings in a card's story, I'm so pleased I looked at Richard and his son. There's a real sense of nostalgia thinking about those old TV programmes, and discovering a connection to iconic movie stars was a bonus.

S044

Canadian Pacific Railway (Atlantic Steamship Lines) Liverpool

Produced by Pickford's Ltd, Walthamstow

S047

USMSS St Paul

Wednesday 20 July 1910
Urgent
Mr John Levi Berry
6 Trinity Road
Wood Green
London N
England

Dear John
Just come from Chicago. I could not go to …
It is a wonderful place. They live in the country … Nebraska.
Was the oil painting sold if so let Esther have 1/2 and keep 1/2 if not 3/6 to pay for it
they will pay you the money John.
Cheer your mother up. How is baby? "Hello dearie"
Get those books away from 7 Park [Avenue] if not sold.
Best love Daddy
I have not had clothes off yet.
3,200 miles by water. It was lovely on the water. I am travelling day and night in the train.
Ticket did not allow for food only on the ship. I hope you've had some good collecting days.
I have written to Dad. We have to wait 8 hours for a train. Only one train a day. Best
love to Lizzie and yourself. Don't leave your place whatever you do.
From J Berry, c/o ? Sandy City, Salt Lake, Utah, USA

The story of this postcard is possibly easier to share by beginning with John Levi Berry's mother, Drusilla née Newell, who was born in Hampshire in 1866. In 1884 she married John Berry, who sent the postcard and who mentions her in the message dated 1910.

In 1901, she appears in records away from her children – John Levi and two daughters, Ada and Abigail. The three children are with their father in Islington.

By 1911, John Levi is a boot shop assistant and living with his stepmother, Esther née Cheeseman, and two half-sisters. John senior had travelled to America and sent his son the postcard. When he and Esther married in 1908, his status is widower. However, Drusilla was definitely alive and didn't die until 1919. Her probate records show that she was a widow and that probate was granted to John Levi Berry, boot shop manager.

Esther and her two daughters sailed to America aboard SS *St Louis* in the summer of 1911 and they eventually joined John in Utah. John and Esther would have more children together – and one son was named Washington Robert Lincoln. John had become a naturalised citizen two years before his son's birth and clearly embraced his new country's history.

Had John and Drusilla divorced? It's unlikely – divorces were becoming more common but were still out of the reach of most people. I came across one family tree created by a direct descendant of John in America where they had added a note about the issue with dates – that Drusilla was alive when John married for the second time. Their comment was that it was 'strange'. They had included all the details from John's first marriage, including the date when Drusilla died. They also had photographs of John Levi and his family, so they were definitely part of the family group, even across the Atlantic.

John had a number of different jobs over the years and another curious element to his story is how his age varies. He was born in 1863 and Esther, his second wife, was born more than 20 years later – a year before John Levi. By the time of the 1920 US census, he had chopped 12 years off his age but when he died in 1943, his age was recorded correctly – his death certificate shows he was 80. Esther had died in 1927.

S110

Feeding Time at the Californian Alligator Farm, Los Angeles

We visited this farm the other day. Rather a novel idea, is it not?

Posted to Devon.

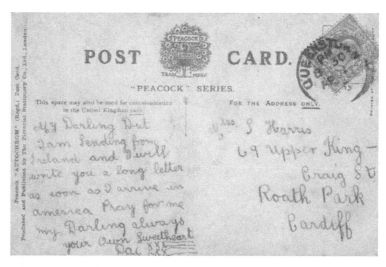

S034

RMS Oceanic

April 1906
Miss S Harris
69 Upper King Craig [Kincraig] *Street*
Roath Park
Cardiff

My Darling Dut [someone who is sweet or cute]
I am sending [this] *from Ireland and I will write you a long letter as soon as I arrive in America.*
Pray for me my Darling, always your own sweetheart.
Dai
XXX
XXX

According to the passenger lists, David Hussey arrived in America in April 1906. The records show that he was married and that he had a brother, Charles, in Ansonia, Connecticut. However, when I found Susannah Harris in Cardiff, she and David didn't marry until the following year. In 1911, her parents (Daniel and Susannah) lived at the address on the card.

David didn't have a brother named Charles but his father did and that brother had emigrated in 1880. In 1890 Charles lived in Ansonia with his wife, Hannah, and worked as a blacksmith.

When David and Susannah married, the register shows him as a bachelor. In 1911 the couple lived in Cardiff where he worked as an engineer with Cardiff Railway. Fortunately, as head of the household, David had completed the census return and that handwriting is a match for that on the postcard – confirming I had followed the correct family.

I don't know why the details in the passenger lists aren't correct – was it easier for a 'married' man to get a passage? Did the immigration authorities consider there was more chance of a person settling in America if they already had a family member there? It isn't always necessary for me to buy certificates but in this case, I decided it would be useful to see David and Susannah's marriage certificate. Unsurprisingly, it showed that David was definitely a bachelor in 1907.

Until 1901, RMS *Oceanic* was the largest ship in the world. Like many others, she was converted into an armed merchant cruiser and commissioned by the Royal Navy in 1914. Her service was short – in September of that year she sailed to patrol the waters off the Shetland Islands and ran aground.

arrived Colombo today leaving tomorrow & all being well should be home a few days after you receive this card. Your mother & Rosemary complain of mal de mer j. a. etc.

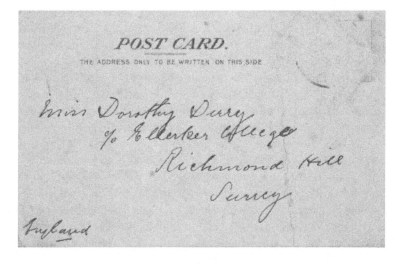

POST CARD.

THE ADDRESS ONLY TO BE WRITTEN ON THIS SIDE

Miss Dorothy Derry
℅ Ellerker College
Richmond Hill
Surrey

England

S036

SS Sunda

Miss Dorothy Derry
C/o Ellerker College
Richmond Hill, Surrey, England

Arrived Colombo today, leaving tomorrow and all being well should be home a few days
after you receive this card. Your mother and Rosemary complain of mal de mer.
y.a. [yours affectionately]

Ellerker College was a school for 'daughters of gentlemen', and although it's not possible to confirm when the postcard was actually sent, Dorothy's year of birth – 1897 – provides some guidance. According to the current occupants, it was originally built as the family home of the first Governor of the Bank of England – Sir John Houblon.

In 1911, Dorothy was living with her parents, Robert and Margaret, as boarders, in Mortlake Road, Kew. Robert was employed within the Colonial Government Service. Dorothy and her brother, Robert junior, were both born abroad in the Federated Malay States. Rosemary, who according to the postcard was suffering from seasickness, was born in Surrey and was seven years younger than Dorothy. In 1896, Robert had married Margaret Lawrie, the daughter of an engineer from Kent. One of several siblings, she had a brother, Peter, who became a mechanical superintendent, working in Penang, Malaysia.

Looking at Robert senior's career, the location of their lodgings in Kew comes as no surprise. He worked overseas for many years (with his family), including in Malacca, and is listed as a member of staff for the Royal (Botanic) Gardens, Kew. Their archives contain letters written to and from Robert while he was abroad, together with notebooks showing lists of plants in his own handwriting. He was Superintendent of Forests in both Malacca and Perak and also Curator at the Botanic Gardens in Singapore. Other correspondence about Robert comments that 'Derry is going home after doing some orchid collecting. The office there is grumbling about Derry not using the billets offered to him'. In 1905, a letter mentions that 'Derry's wife brought back the smallpox and is very ill; Derry and his children are quarantined'.

Robert and Margaret's son, Robert junior, would continue his father's work – in the Indian Forest Service in a conservation role. He married in India in 1927. When his wife died in 1948, he is included in the probate records as an Indian government official. Dorothy married Henry Humphreys, an actuary from Chadwell Heath, Essex and the couple lived in Twickenham.

Exploring archives – either in person or via online catalogues – certainly added to this card's story. Reading that the family were affected by smallpox, and knowing that they all survived, was fascinating.

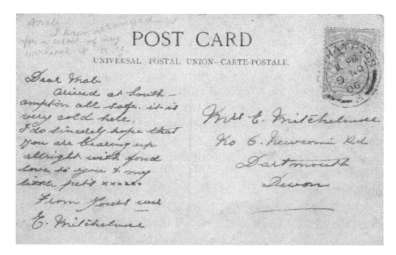

S032

SS St Louis

With fondest love, Ern

9 November 1906
Mrs E Mitchelmore
No 6 Newcomen Road
Dartmouth
Devon

Dear Mab
Arrived at Southampton all safe. It is very cold here.
I do sincerely hope that you are bearing up alright.
With fond love to you and my little pets.
XXXXXX
From yours ever
E Mitchelmore
Mab
I have arranged for a letter of my arrival at NY

It wasn't necessarily unusual for a husband to travel across the Atlantic alone – perhaps to seek work and to establish himself before his wife and family joined him. Was this why Alfred Ernest Mitchelmore travelled without his wife, Mabel, and their young children? His visit to America was extended – he didn't return until August 1907.

According to the passenger lists for the ship, Alfred declared that he knew Frederick Pillar in America. Like Alfred, Frederick was also born in Dartmouth; he lived in America with his Iowa-born wife, Olive. He had emigrated in 1889 and became a naturalised citizen 11 years later. With his wife and daughter, Frederick appears in passenger lists returning to England several times. He died in Denver, Colorado in the 1930s.

Frederick was more than a decade older than Alfred and it's possible that he was friends with Alfred's older brothers as both families lived near to each other. Augustus Mitchelmore was the eldest, born in 1863. According to his Royal Navy records he enlisted as a boy and was relatively short, had dark blue eyes and auburn hair. Later, his occupation is given as shipwright. The 1911 census shows him as an artisan carpenter, serving in the Mediterranean. Two years later he was appointed Chief Carpenter of Hong Kong Dockyard. Immediately after the First World War he was awarded the MBE for *valuable services in carrying out repairs to the vessels of the Sixth Destroyer Flotilla.* Other records add: *This officer has had an exceptional amount of extra work caused by enemy action and collision casualties, and by his energy and zeal has on many occasions reduced the periods of vessels being out of action. The high state of efficiency of the Dover Patrol Destroyers is due in a large extent to the good work of Shipwright Lieutenant Mitchelmore.*

Alfred's wife, Mabel née Beadon, also had siblings who were sailors. John lost his life in 1916 when SS *Lorca* was hit by a torpedo and the crew of more than 30 were lost. In 1927, Frank Beadon was second mate of the cargo ship SS *Emlynmor*. The ship was last seen off Beachy Head in heavy weather with the loss of all men.

It isn't known what motivated Alfred Mitchelmore to travel to America. After he returned to his wife, the couple and their growing family remained in Devon.

S000

*In fine remembrance of your dear brother Fred, who leaves for
China today 1 October 1909.
May God bless and comfort him while he is away and
trust he will return safe.*

Posted to Ramsgate in 1909.

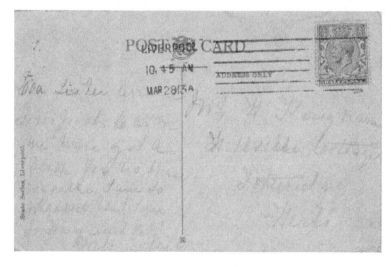

S012

RMS Victorian

28 March 1913
Mr H Kingham
Hillside Cottage
Totteridge, Hertfordshire

Dear Sister and all
… We have got a berth for us three together. I am so pleased.
Best love to all and self
Will &Lottie

Sometimes it seems as if searching for passengers on a ship is an easy stage in the process of revealing a postcard's story. This postcard was beset with problems – caused mainly by poorly scanned documents, smudged writing and transcription errors. However, through a process of elimination, and a little luck, I was able to confirm that the postcard was sent by William Kingham who was on the ship with his wife, Charlotte, and their young granddaughter, Vera Williams, who shared a cabin with her grandparents. It was Vera's entry that led to the confirmation of her grandparents' identity as her name, thankfully, appeared next to their incorrectly transcribed names – from the card's message I knew I was looking for three people in one cabin.

Vera was born in 1902 and her mother was Mabel, Charlotte's daughter from her first marriage, to John Button. After his death in 1885, Charlotte married William Kingham in 1900.

Vera's father was Edward Williams, a railway engineer who began his employment at the age of 14 as an apprentice. In 1908, Edward was working in Nyasaland (Malawi) for the Shire Highlands Railway. In April of that year he was stricken with blackwater fever, a form of malaria, which ultimately led to heart failure. He was treated in the Railway Hospital in Chiromo where his death was registered.

By 1920, William, Charlotte and Vera were living in Washington State and with them were Frank and George, two of Charlotte's sons. The postcard was sent to William's brother, Henry. He lived at the address with his wife, Maria.

As well as a nice piece of detective work, this card's a lovely example of how some research really can't tell the full story. Why did William and Charlotte decide to emigrate and why did Mabel send her little girl to America? Mabel died just a few months short of her hundredth birthday – in England.

RMS *Victorian* was another ship used during the First World War and was the world's first turbine-powered ocean liner, working as a mail ship for the Allan Line. During the First World War the ship was an armed merchant cruiser and ultimately carried cargo and troops.

S007

*RPD R*oon

21 May 1904
Mrs McCheane
The Cottage , Adel, Nr Leeds, England

This is just to send you a line and thank you very much for your letter. This is to be posted
at Gibraltar tomorrow. It is a lovely day.
RVT May 20 1904

Emma Horsfall married James McCheane in 1862 when she was 19. James
was a vicar and the couple had one daughter, Ethel. Emma's father, Abraham
Horsfall, was a solicitor and the family lived in the Manor House, Whitkirk.
In recent years, Leeds Civic Trust has attached a blue plaque to the building,
commemorating John Wesley preaching in its garden. Emma's brother, John,
became a surgeon and worked for a time in Bournemouth, Dorset (then
Hampshire) and some records show that he died in Naples in 1904. James
McCheane died in 1881, at the age of 46. His daughter, Ethel, would serve as
a nurse during the First World War.

Searching through the passenger lists for the German ship RPD *Roon*, I
hoped to find someone whose initials matched those on the postcard and the
only contender was a Miss R Teale. However, there were no other details to
help identify her; all I knew was that she was on her way to Shanghai.

As I returned to Emma's family, I discovered her mother's maiden name
was Teale. Mary Teale was born in 1808, making it difficult to discover her
siblings. However, I did confirm that she had a brother named Thomas,
whose granddaughter was Renee Verena Teale, born in 1875. Renee appears
in census returns as a teacher, including in 1911 in Wantage, Berkshire. The
1939 register records her at St Mark's Mission House, Wiltshire as a Church
of England nun.

Her father was Thomas Teale, a surgeon – as was her grandfather and
great-grandfather. Other members of the family were also doctors. Her father
was president of the Leeds Philosophical and Literary Society and according
to an online biography he was: *one of the oldest men to serve in the British Army in*
the First World War. He was 83 when he was called up in August 1914, and 87 at the
time of his discharge. He served as a Lt Colonel in the Royal Army Medical Corps.

Renee appears in a 1905 *Directory of Protestant Missionaries in China, Japan*
and Korea. The directory has advertisements, including one for the missionary
home in Shanghai where devotional books, stationery, typewriters and the
Estey organ – 'the most popular for missionary uses, being acclimatised and
sold at the lowest prices' – were available.

Renee died in the 1950s at a convent in Wantage.

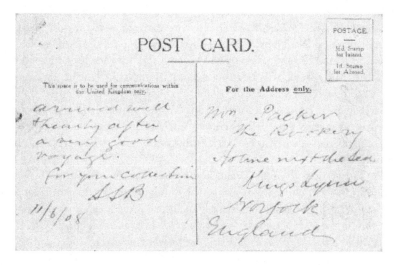

S041

RMS Lusitania

11 June 08
Mrs Packer
The Rookery
Holme-next-the-Sea
Kings Lynn
Norfolk
England

Arrived well and hearty after a very good voyage.
For your collection.
SSB

Although Samuel Stanley Brown frequently crossed the Atlantic for business, he wasn't sailing on RMS *Lusitania* when he sent the postcard. He arrived in Boston on 11 June 1908, having sailed on SS *Ivernia*. This ship, like *Lusitania*, was torpedoed during the First World War. Thirty-six crew and 84 of the estimated 2,400 troops she was carrying lost their lives.

Samuel's 1908 sailing wasn't his first on *Ivernia* – he sailed on her in 1904. It was possible to track Samuel sailing to America regularly and he also sailed to Canada aboard RMS *Empress of Britain* the following year. As 'Brown' is a common name, confirming Samuel's occupation and home addresses was crucial in eliminating trips by other Browns.

In 1911, Samuel lived with his wife, Hannah née Packer, in Dulwich and his employment is given as manager of an insurance company. In 1901, he and Hannah lived with Ellen Packer at the address on the card. Ellen née Manlove had married Samuel Packer in 1867 – Hannah's brother. The Packer family were from Nottingham and Samuel Packer was a lace manufacturer. Their son, Gilbert, became a lace draughtsman. Another son, Harry, became a doctor.

S048

SS Suevic

25 May 1907
Mr TE Chantry
Airmyn Grange
Goole
Yorkshire
England

Dear Uncle
Have had very bad weather. We met the Midi but being late did not stop to take our meals.
Hope to get to Cape Town Friday.

Thomas Chantry was a farmer who was born in Selby, Yorkshire. In 1875 he married farmer's daughter Ellen Baxter and the couple would have at least ten children. One son, Harold, was a bank clerk and in 1911, he worked in Broughton and boarded with the Barnes family who were market gardeners. In 1914, Harold married Mina Hugill and a few months later they appear in passenger lists sailing on RMS *Lusitania* to America and then travelling on to Canada where their daughter, Ellen, was born. In May the following year, the family planned to return to England – again sailing on *Lusitania*.

Passengers were warned of the dangers of crossing the Atlantic; they would be sailing through a war zone. The ship was hit by a torpedo off the coast of Ireland and following an explosion, sank within minutes. Harold, Mina and Ellen were all killed and the research of others links them to a mention in AA Hoehling and Mary Hoehling's book, *The Last Voyage of the Lusitania*. The book, published in 1956, is written in a similar style to Walter Lord's *A Night to Remember* – blending narrative with factual research. The *Lusitania* book says: *a mother from Third, with her baby and her emaciated husband who seemed to be suffering with tuberculosis, came over ... she was advised to strap the baby in front of her ... the sickly husband appeared frightened.* Perhaps from the description of the husband, it is possible that Harold could be identified – his family may have known that he was ill.

So many of the stories and families I research are connected – by coincidence and fate – and in the story of *Lusitania*, there is 'almost' a connection to both RMS *Titanic* and RMS *Empress of Ireland*. Fireman Frank Tower is mentioned in the *Lusitania* book as having survived all three tragedies. However, other researchers cite that no one named Frank Tower appears in the relevant crew records and that folklore has turned the story into fact – which is then repeated by the Hoehlings.

There is a connection, however, between SS *Suevic* and *Titanic* – it was onboard *Suevic* in 1903 that a young officer, Charles Lightoller, met his future wife. Charles was the most senior member of *Titanic*'s crew to survive the sinking.

In 1907, *Suevic* was sailing from Australia to England and encountered treacherous weather conditions off the coast of Cornwall and eventually ran aground. Ultimately, five RNLI lifeboats reached the stricken ship and began removing passengers and crew, taking them ashore to safety. For 16 hours, the volunteers sailed to and from the ship and eventually 456 lives were saved, including 70 babies. For their bravery, six Silver Medals for Gallantry were awarded by the RNLI to their crew members, and also to two members of the *Suevic* crew.

Thomas Chantry, who received the card, had several siblings and it wasn't possible to identify who sent the card to their uncle.

S081

RMS Lusitania and Mauretania

'Good old Ireland' to give us a smooth hour or two after a windy night.
Breakfast will be ready in a few minutes and I feel quite ready for it now.

Posted to York in 1910.

S074

Slip Way, Lifeboat House and Coastguards Station, Cromer

12 August 1907
Mr Dolbear
35 The Broadway
Cricklewood
London NW

Dear F & M
We are enjoying our holiday, weather fine, return next Friday. Hoping you are well.
With love from us all.
Fred

Fred Dolbear was likely on holiday with his wife, Eliza, and their children. Fred worked for the GPO as a sorter and his father, Fred senior, was a painter and decorator. By 1911 Fred senior had retired from that trade but worked as a church officer with the Presbyterian church in Willesden. He had at least nine children with his wife, Jane née Bond, including Harry who was born in 1867, two years after Fred. Harry was a seaman in the Royal Navy and in 1891 he served on HMS *Vernon* – a torpedo ship. Twenty years later he was a torpedo gunner with the Royal Navy.

When I decided to include a postcard that linked directly with the RNLI, I was overwhelmed with the choice – but I chose this particular card simply because I liked the image. Once I had confirmed the details for the Dolbear family, I had a look at the Cromer lifeboat station and came across a fascinating story of bravery. In all honesty, all of our RNLI lifeboat stations would reveal stories of bravery. In Swanage, where I grew up, there are generations of families that have served and continue to serve – putting their own lives at risk.

When my maternal grandfather, Alfred Tatchell, sailed to Larne from Stranraer in 1953 aboard MV *Princess Victoria*, he lost his life – caught by bad luck in a storm that would eventually work its way to the east coast of England and wreak havoc and destruction, and a great loss of life in the ensuing floods. *Princess Victoria* was a ferry, setting sail in atrocious conditions in a sea that would breach its doors. Those doors weren't closed properly – something today's technology would control. My grandfather was one of the 133 who lost their lives and I'm beyond grateful to those, including the brave RNLI volunteers, who risked their own lives in trying to save him and the other passengers and crew.

Before Henry Blogg retired in 1947, having served on Cromer's lifeboats for 53 years, he had helped to save 873 lives. Henry grew up in Cromer and left school at the age of 11 to work with his family on the beach and in their crabbing boat. Seven years later he joined the lifeboat crew and eventually became coxswain. During that time he received several Gold and Silver Medals from the RNLI, the George Cross (awarded for his work during the

Second World War) and a British Empire Medal – all resulting in him being the most decorated person in the RNLI's history.

Members of the Donaghadee lifeboat station in Northern Ireland were awarded medals for their efforts during the attempted rescue of MV *Princess Victoria*. In Swanage, five Silver and five Bronze Medals have been presented – the first in 1839.

S022

With no message on the reverse, Arthur was clearly a man of few words!

Posted in 1906 to Arthur's sister, Bessie, in Poole.

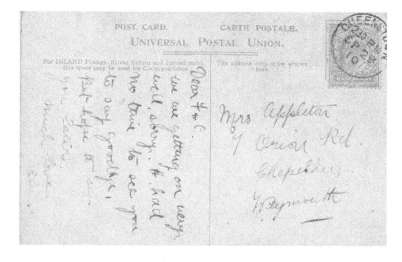

S070

RMS Majestic

29 September 1910
Mrs Appleton
7 Orion Road
Chapelhey, Weymouth

Dear F & C
We are getting on very well. Sorry H had no time to see you to say goodbye. But hope to see you later.
Much love.
E…

Carlton Appleton was born in Scarborough in 1879 and he worked at the torpedo factory at the Isle of Portland near Weymouth as an engineer's turner. He married Flora Nicholson in 1902 and the couple would eventually move to Rochester where Flora worked as a nursing sister.

Carlton's brother, Leonard, began his career as a manufacturer's clerk and eventually became building manager in Bournville, taking responsibility for the ongoing development of the village, owned by the Cadbury family. By 1939 he was secretary and manager for the estate. His wife, Norah née Ingoldby, was born in London but after the death of both her parents, she lived with her uncle in Weymouth. Henry 'H' Syms had a business in St Thomas Street and he sailed on RMS *Majestic* with his wife, Emma, and their two children. Emma's signature when she married Henry is a perfect match to the writing on the card – especially the 'M' (her middle name was Marianne) used for 'Mrs'.

Carlton and Leonard's father was a grocer and storekeeper for an asylum in Kings Norton. He married Mary Pegler in 1869. As a child she had attended Ackworth School, a Quaker school near Pontefract – as did the couple's children. The archives at the school contain detailed information about the family including photographs of the children taken outside the school with their classmates.

Knowing what Carlton did as a job raises questions about his religion – at least in later years. Helping to build torpedoes seems an unlikely job for Carlton – and talking with Quakers today, they think it unlikely that he had remained a Quaker. Leonard served in the First World War in the Royal Army Service Corps, perhaps in a non-fighting capacity. Carlton was a Royal Navy reservist. Living in Weymouth and working at the nearby torpedo factory meant he would have been acutely aware of the risks to the area during the war. *Weymouth, Dorchester & Portland in the Great War*, by Jacqueline Wadsworth, mentions that Carl Lody, a German naval officer and spy, was spotted (although not apprehended) in the seaside town. Posing as an American tourist, he left the area and was eventually captured in Edinburgh and executed at the Tower of London.

S102

Ascent of the great Pyramid

1908
Master Vernon Blamey
Acosta Villa
Hayle
Cornwall
England

Hearty congratulations on your passing the music exam.
Fond love to you from Father.

Vernon was 14 years old when his father sent the postcard from Egypt. Although it's impossible to know with certainty why William, Vernon's father, was in Egypt, he was certainly a well-travelled person. When he married Ada Uren in 1888, his occupation was engineer. His father, William senior, was a mine captain and agent who had worked abroad – William junior was born in Mexico.

In 1881, young William was a boarder at Hart House School in Tregony, Cornwall. His mother, Amelia, was no stranger to the workings of a mine – her father, Francis Blamey (a distant relative of William's) was also a copper miner as were other members of the family.

In 1911, Vernon's father appears in records as an engineer in Dartmouth. He lived with his wife's sister and her husband, Thomas Hodge, who was an engine fitter 'in the making of torpedoes'. At this time, Vernon was living with his mother and younger brother, known as Lance, at the postcard's address and they were farmers.

X This is NOT my bedroom window ?!!!

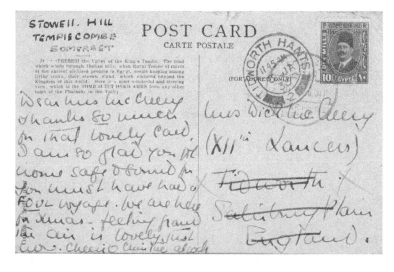

S106

The Valley of the King's Tombs (Thebes)

Mrs Dick McCreery
(XIIth Lancers)
~~*Tidworth*~~
~~*Salisbury Plain*~~
England
Stowell Hill
Templecombe
Somerset

Dear Mrs McCreery
Thanks so much for that lovely card. I am so glad you are home safe and sound from your visit. Have had a __foul__ voyage. We are here for Xmas – feeling grand, the air is lovely just now. Cheerio.

X This is __NOT__ my bedroom windows?!!!

Lettice St Maur was the daughter of Major Lord Percy St Maur (younger brother of the 15th Duke of Somerset). When she married Richard McCreery in 1928, a newspaper reported that she entered the church in London not with a traditional bouquet, but a prayer book in one hand and her dog, sporting a blue bow, under her arm. Principal guests included the Duke and Duchess of Somerset (her grandparents), Lord and Lady Seymour and the Duchess of Norfolk. The Seymour family (holders of the dukedom) are perhaps best known in Tudor history from the marriage of Jane Seymour to Henry VIII. Richard McCreery's father was an American citizen who was born in Switzerland in 1871. Although he spent many years in England, he represented the United States at polo at the 1900 Summer Olympics.

Richard's full title was General Sir Richard Loudon McCreery, GCB, KBE, DSO, MC. In 1915, he was commissioned as a second lieutenant into the The Prince of Wales' Royal Lancers and eventually arrived in France in January 1916. A few months later he was shot in his right thigh, severing his femoral artery. Although the immediate treatment helped to reduce the blood loss, it led to gangrene in his foot and it was feared his leg would be amputated. However, he 'only' lost two toes and parts of the others. After his recovery he continued to serve, and in the final days of the war he led his squadron in a mounted attack on a German machine gun post, capturing ten prisoners and a machine gun in the process. The recommendation was that he be awarded the Military Cross for 'valuable and dashing work when in command of a mounted patrol'.

Richard served in Italy during the Second World War and it is reported that he was knighted 'in the field' in July 1944 by King George VI, at Palazzo del Pero, Italy.

Despite the injuries sustained during the First World War which left him with a pronounced limp, he was an accomplished horseman. His steeplechasing skills were commemorated in an annual race at Sandown Park, The Dick McCreery Hunters' Chase.

At the Coronation of Queen Elizabeth II in 1953, the State Coach was drawn by six horses, one of which was named McCreery, the others being named after five other Second World War generals.

Richard's mother was Emilia McAdam, great-great-granddaughter of the Scottish engineer John Loudon McAdam (born in 1756), who was famous for his invention of the process of 'Macadamisation', a method of road surfacing. Emilia's great-grandfather was James Nicoll McAdam, known to his contemporaries as 'The Colossus of Roads'. Many of us will have learned about the McAdam family's contribution to our roads at school – I certainly remember those lessons as among my favourites.

S109

Panama Canal

Posted in 1916 in America.

MOONLIGHT SCENE OF THE FORUM (COOK'S TEN GUINEA ROME TOURS)

S099

Moonlight scene of the Forum (Cook's ten guinea Rome tours)

JH Stanton Esq
Stubb House
Winston
Darlington

John Stanton was an engineer who was born in the late 1830s in Newcastle. In 1859 he married Elizabeth Bidder, who was ten years his junior. Elizabeth's father was George Bidder, known in his youth as 'Calculating Boy'. In Moretonhampstead in Devon, George's father exploited his son's gift of being able to make instant calculations in his head. Together, they would visit events and George senior charged a fee to anyone wishing to see his son 'perform'. Fortunately, perhaps through good luck, he came under the patronage of George Stephenson with whom he eventually worked – George Stephenson would become Elizabeth's godfather. George Bidder could, it's recorded, look at the engineering drawings of a project and recognise almost immediately if a calculation had been made incorrectly.

George Bidder and his wife, Georgina Harby, were untypical of Victorian parents. Elizabeth was encouraged to be inquisitive and was educated far beyond her contemporaries might expect. In 1858, at the age of 18, she was invited to join Robert Stephenson and his party to sail on his schooner *The Titania* to Egypt. Elizabeth's journey to Egypt began at Southampton in the middle of October. Fortunately, she kept a detailed diary – of the yacht's location, the weather and anything that occurred of interest.

In the Bay of Biscay the weather was unfavourable – washing was managed, she wrote, *by sitting on the floor beside my bath, but then came the hair – the looking glass in my cabin was on the windward side … after about ten minutes … a sudden lurch sent me spinning onto the sofa.* Elizabeth was a plucky sort and ventured out onto the deck wearing a borrowed tarpaulin coat; *the captain seized a rope and lashed me to the side much to my amusement.*

Elizabeth recorded the anecdotes of those in the party, including Robert Stephenson recounting a tale from his childhood. Having read of Benjamin Franklin's electrical kite, *he could never rest until he possessed one. Using savings from his pocket money, he bought a wire string. The experiment succeeded admirably and he amused himself by electrifying everyone he could entice into his room.*

The journey to Egypt was made during relatively relaxed times and at Gibraltar, the 'gentlemen' visited the Consul to enquire if passports would be required – none were. Towards the end of November, Elizabeth awoke in her cabin to a *deluge of water reaching even into my bed, my slippers … were floating about like two boats … Happily Mr Stephenson was on the weather side or he says he thinks he would have been floated out of bed.*

By the end of November, the party reached Alexandria, visiting a number of sights including Cleopatra's Needle. A conversation over dinner prompted some of the ladies to have their eyes outlined in kohl by a local woman who visited them with *an elegant little gold bottle filled with kohl and some straws ... we knelt down and* [it was] *put into our eyes ... rather a painful operation and one that made the tears run down my cheeks.* Elizabeth's eyes were washed with rose water and another, this time successful, attempt was achieved.

A week later, Elizabeth rode by donkey to visit the pyramids – thirty miles from her Cairo hotel and a journey of about two hours. After a break, some of the group were guided inside – Elizabeth's dress was 'inconvenient' and tied like a shawl round her waist. She stooped through the entrance and describes in her diary the method of entry: *an Arab seizes each hand and half leads and half carries you up another long steep slippery plane* [of about seven feet]. Eventually she was obliged to creep *almost on hands and knees, then you are swung over a shaft...* And so it continued until she reached the King's chamber. The exit was no less easy, but she was *glad to reach the fresh air, half-baked, dusty and cramped.* Next, with Robert Stephenson, came the ascent of the pyramid. With three guides each, they eventually reached the summit and its magnificent views.

On 20 December, Elizabeth mentions Robert visiting Isambard Kingdom Brunel, who had arrived a few days earlier, in poor health, with his wife and son. Elizabeth spent time with Mrs Brunel, although she found her as *stiff as a poker.* On Christmas Day, Elizabeth's group visited the Brunels' hotel where they ate their dinner together.

'Mr Stanton' (her future husband) is mentioned many times throughout the stay in Egypt in very factual terms. Perhaps she decided to keep her feelings private and away from anyone who might read her diary.

Elizabeth and the group eventually returned to England aboard a steamer and her parents met her, with some relief I expect, in France.

A few months later George Bidder sailed his own yacht, *The Mayfly*, to Norway where Robert Stephenson was the recipient of the Knight Grand Cross of the Order of St Olaf (one of many international awards he received). His health had not been good for many months and he died shortly after this final trip, nursed (so it is recorded in Elizabeth's diary) by her mother to the end.

In 1861, Anthony Trollope published a collection of short stories, *Tales of All Countries*, and included 'An Unprotected Female At The Pyramids' which describes how a party from Cairo travelled by donkey, entered a pyramid's base and then later climbed to the summit – *this entrance into the Pyramids is a terrible task, which should be undertaken by no lady ... Those who perform it have to creep down, and then to be dragged up, through infinite dirt, foul smells, and bad air; and when they have done it, they see nothing.* Clearly Trollope had never met Elizabeth!

Whether Elizabeth and John Stanton had met before her journey isn't known with certainty. He was working in Egypt for Robert Stephenson and perhaps their paths hadn't yet crossed. Just a few months after her return, in the autumn of 1859, the couple married. It was a subdued event – they were still in mourning for Robert Stephenson who had died just a few weeks earlier.

The couple had a large family of at least 12 children. I came across a mention of one of their daughters, Dorothy, in an online local history book published in Canada. Dorothy married Ogilvy Forde (who was born in Ireland). He had travelled to Canada, chasing the Klondike Gold Rush, and eventually settled on Vancouver Island where he met Dorothy. The book's excerpt says that she had left England because she was *impatient with the old custom of having daughters marry in order of age ... Dorothy left for Vancouver Island* (where a brother had settled). Ogilvy wanted to move to another area and eventually, having decided on what seems like an adventure Elizabeth would have enjoyed, sent for Dorothy and they were married. With others, they headed for Francois Lake in British Columbia where a raft was made. During the journey, Dorothy made sails from the wagon's covers. The couple eventually settled in a remote area where their groceries arrived every six months on horseback.

John Stanton's postcard was bought because Rome is one of my favourite cities; I knew that I could trace him and that he was an engineer – that's all. I had no idea where his story would lead me. This has been an excellent adventure!

Elizabeth's diary is held by the Robert Stephenson Trust who graciously allowed me to quote the extracts here. You can read the full diary via their website – RobertStephensonTrust.com.

S024

Did you spot any secret messages sent with the postcards?!

Postscript

I'm often asked at talks, how I began researching postcards. If you've read either of my earlier books, you'll know this story – but perhaps you won't know what happened more recently.

Many years ago, my parents bought a postcard at a car boot sale. Dad chose it for its stamp – the card was sent from America to a Grenadier Guard in the Chelsea Barracks. Over the years that followed, I researched the short life of Gilbert Freeman who was killed in the Battle of the Somme. He had been fighting for friends and family, for King and country – and for future generations, people like us, so it seemed a natural act of remembrance to research and share his story. I discovered that Gilbert's two brothers had emigrated from Saltash in Cornwall to America – Dad's postcard had been sent by one of those brothers – and I was amazed when a granddaughter in America contacted me on Facebook. They had come across some of the information I'd shared online and it was one of those moments that rely so much on chance – them looking, just hours after I'd uploaded the story, and earlier, that postcard being found by someone who would ultimately be interested enough to discover more.

Years later, as I shared in *Second Delivery*, I came across another postcard connected to Gilbert's family – a coincidence that will always send shivers up my spine. Searching for a postcard of Minehead to use in a talk, I came across a card of Saltash sent to one of Gilbert's brothers at the army camp in Minehead. The seller of the card had included the recipient's details which is why a postcard of Saltash appeared in a search for Minehead. I can't help feeling I was meant to find that card.

It's impossible to say that a research project is complete and that's definitely true with Gilbert's story. In early 2023, I was giving a Zoom talk to a family history group and during the Q&As, someone told me about an Order of Service from February 1919 that had been kept by their grandfather who had attended the service held at St Paul's Cathedral. During the talk, I'd noticed this person reaching out to the side and they said they'd been grabbing the book because only that morning they'd been looking at it.

There are more than 120 pages in the book (it's not an Order of Service of just a few pages that many of us will be familiar with). It lists all the Guardsmen who had been killed in the First World War up until December 1918 when it was published (there's a note inside explaining that more names would be added to a separate cover in due course). During my talk, the person checked the lists and found Gilbert. Later, I managed to buy a copy myself and when it arrived I found that a past custodian had included newspaper clippings for 20 or so of the men killed – in memoriam notices, articles from local magazines, etc. I immediately decided that I would add the details for Gilbert and include this update when I next gave a talk that includes his postcard.

The Order of Service generates a lot of interest and I'm sometimes asked to check for names. Later, I've invited these people to send me short biographies about their Guardsmen who lost their lives and so the information continues to grow.

I don't think I've ever given a talk where there hasn't been at least one person mention a collection of postcards that they've inherited. These people rightly regard them as heirlooms. They tell a story, perhaps several, revealing what their ancestors were doing, where they were visiting, what grumbles they had. Others have told me of cards bought because the image connects with their family's roots – and then, after my talk, have explored the story 'behind' the cards. Of course, you do need access to genealogy resources to fully reveal these stories, but often there are 'free to access' records that can help begin the journey.

The number of postcards being sent each year is dropping – the cost of sending them is prohibitive and they can take days to be delivered. Similarly, many of us opt for online greetings, especially at Christmas and for birthdays. How long will it be before we no longer know the handwriting of our friends and family?

Nostalgia is one of the reasons people collect postcards – we often have a need to reflect on our earlier years and attach affection to even the mundane. A postcard of a street where you lived, a shop where you bought sweets could be the beginning of your own collection. Hunting out the cards that follow a particular theme is all part of the attraction. You might prefer to pay more than is strictly necessary to have a mint card, or perhaps you'll go for the creased and torn ones, the cards that have been posted, handled and enjoyed.

You will have noticed that some of my cards in this book are extremely tatty. They were mainly sent before the First World War – a period regarded as the 'golden era' of sending postcards. At this time it was cheaper to send a postcard than a letter – and if you lived in a larger town or city, postboxes would be emptied several times a day from just after six in the morning through to eight at night. That meant that the message was likely to arrive the same day – an affordable way to keep in touch with people who lived relatively nearby. Many of the cards were produced in Germany, so the outbreak of war affected the supply. Also, in the years that followed, the cost of sending a card increased to match that of sending a letter. Still, there's no shortage of cards to buy, and although I prefer to buy older ones, some of the cards sent before the Second World War are every bit as interesting. Of course, I continue to add to my own collection – why would I stop? Sometimes I need a particular image to illustrate something I'm either talking or writing about. Sometimes I just want to enjoy searching for the unexpected.

I do hope you've enjoyed reading this collection of stories – and that perhaps it's even inspired you to have a rummage in a junk shop's box of ephemera. I'm indebted to the people who wrote the cards and sent them – and to those who received and saved those brief messages. The cards I have researched and included in my books, articles or talks have found their way to me by chance and good fortune, and I'm extremely grateful for the way in which they've reached me.

Index

About the
Author

Helen Baggott is a speaker and author from Dorset. Her passion is researching the stories behind postcards sent more than a hundred years ago. So far, three collections of stories have been published as *Posted in the Past*, *Posted in the Past Second Delivery*, and *Posted in the Past Hands Across the Sea*.

She has written for regional magazines; national magazines include *This England*, *Discover Your Ancestors*, *Who Do You Think You Are?*, *Picture Postcard Monthly* and *The Card Scene*. She has also written for *Family Tree* magazine's blog. Her work has been recognised by national newspapers as both a Postcard and Heirloom Detective.

Through the power of Zoom she speaks to groups on both sides of the Atlantic and in Australia. She has been a speaker at the Family History Federation's Really Useful Show, The Genealogy Show and a guest speaker for the Society of Genealogists. Helen usually offers a choice of at least ten talks.

Before she embarks on the next in the *Posted in the Past* series, *Return to Sender*, Helen is releasing a book to raise money for Parkinson's UK – *With Love from Grace*.

In the years before the First World War, Grace travelled Europe with a wealthy Italian family. She visited the Count's homes, stayed in some of the best hotels and regularly sent postcards to Douglas, the man she would eventually marry. More than 80 of those postcards are included in this book. All royalties will be paid to Parkinson's UK. The charity has been chosen because Helen's father suffered from Parkinson's disease.

Contact Helen by email: PostedInThePast@gmail.com
Facebook, Instagram and X (Twitter): @PostedInThePast
#PostedInThePast

Printed in Great Britain
by Amazon

43807677R00119